NEW ROUTES IN GCSE GEOGRAPHY

Across the Developing World

MICHAEL HAIGH

CAMBRIDGE
UNIVERSITY PRESS

Published by the Press Syndicate of the University of Cambridge
The Pitt Building, Trumpington Street, Cambridge CB2 1RP
32 East 57th Street, New York, NY 10022, USA
296 Beaconsfield Parade, Middle Park, Melbourne 3166, Australia

© Cambridge University Press 1984, 1989

First published 1984
Second edition 1988
Reprinted 1993
Printed in Hong Kong by Wing King Tong

Library of Congress catalogue card number: 83--2109

British Library cataloguing in publication data

Haigh, Michael
    Across the developing word--(New routes in geography)
    1. Underdeveloped areas
    I. Title II. Series
    909'.097240828   AC59.7

ISBN 0 521 35781 0

(First edition ISBN 0 521 28631 X)

DPP

Cover photograph: Trans-Andean section of the Pan-American Highway linking Chile and Argentina

Acknowledgements

The author and the publisher would like to thank the following for permission to use copyright photographs:
Centre for World Development Education 4, 82 top; World Bank: Ramon Cerra 6, 7, 10; World Bank: Tomas Sennett 24 bottom, 31, 32 left, 33; World Bank: Ray Witlin 53, 70 bottom, 71 left, 78, 79, 80 top; World Bank: Edwin G. Huffmann 59 top, 60 top, bottom, 61; World Bank: Mary M. Hill back cover, 86 bottom, 87; Unicef 8 top, 56, 67 bottom left, 68 right, 71 top and bottom right, 75 bottom left, 76 bottom, 80 bottom, 81; United Nations 1, 8 bottom, 9, 13 top, 14, 20, 25 bottom, 45, 60 centre, 69, 75 left (Ray Witlin), 112 bottom left, 113 bottom right, 118 bottom left, 119 bottom left; Central Office of Information 11, 18 top, 82 left; Christian Aid 13 bottom, 23 left, 24 top, 25 top, 39 bottom right, 67 right, 68 left, 70 top right, 72, 74 left, top right, 75 top left, 76 top, 120 left, bottom right, 122, 123, 126, 127; Pesco Peru 18 bottom, 19; Inter-American Development Bank front cover, 22, 36; Brazilian Embassy, London 23 right, 27 bottom right, 29, 30, 37, 38, 40, 46; International Coffee Organisation 26, 27 left, top right, 28; Ishikawajima-Harima Heavy Industries Ltd 34, 42; Hitachi Zosen 35; Tourist Development Corporation of Malaysia 39 left, top right, 84, 85, 89, 90, 95; Alcan Smelters and Chemicals Ltd 43; South American Pictures (Tony Morrison) 44; Roan Consolidated Mines Ltd 50 top left, bottom, 51; Trade Commissioner for the Republic of Zambia, London 47, 50 top right, 52; Zambia National Tourist Board 54, 55 left, top right, 57, 59 bottom, 64 bottom, 65, 66; M. Champkin 55 bottom right, 58; The Zambia Sugar Company Ltd 62; J.F. Parsons 67 top left; Oxfam 74 bottom right, 77, 124; Food and Agriculture Organisation 86 top; Malaysian Timber Industry Board 88, 102 left, 107 bottom; Malaysian Rubber Producers' Research Association 91, 92, 94; Office of the High Commissioner for Malaysia 93, 96; Angela Joynson 98, 99, 100, 104 bottom, 106, 107 top; Shell Photo Service 102 right, 103; David Williams 104 bottom right, 112 top, bottom right, 113 top, 114 bottom right, 116 bottom right, 117 bottom left, 119 top; Blue Circle Industries PLC 105 left, 105 top; J. Allan Cash Ltd 104, 108; Mike Wells, Aspect Picture Library 109; Joyce Williams 110 centre right, 111 left, 112 centre right, 114 left, top right, 115 top, bottom right, 116 left, 117 top right, 118 top, 119 bottom right, 120 bottom right; Robert Withnall 110 top, left, 111 right, 113 bottom left, 115 bottom left, 116 top, 117 top left, bottom right, 118 bottom right; War on Want 121, 125.

Contents

Peru	4
Journey to Peru	4
The land of Peru	5
A village in the Andes	8
Lima	11
Irrigating the desert	15
Selling the country's resources	17
Industrial fishing	18
Minerals from the mountains	20
Links across the continent	22

Brazil	23
One-half of South America	23
Poverty in the dry north-east	24
Coffee in Brazil	26
Sao Paulo: fast-growing city	30
Industry in Brazil	32
Multinational companies in Brazil	34
Developing the interior: Brasilia	36
Opening up the forest	39
Roads and farms in the forest	40
Projects in the forest	42
The Amazon Indians	45

Zambia	47
A mining country	47
Routes to the coast	48
A copper mine in Zambia	50
Depending on copper	53
A Zambian village	54
Lusaka: capital city of Zambia	59
Crops for sale	62
A farming future for Zambia	64
Power and industry	65
Wildlife: the struggle for survival	66

India	67
Contrasting landscapes	67
A problem of people	68
Poverty in the countryside	70
Drought, flood and disaster	76
Cities	79
Industry	82

Malaysia	84
A mixture of peoples and places	84
The Malays: poverty in the countryside	85
Tin	89
Rubber	91
Kuala Lumpur: mining camp to primate city	95
New industries for Malaysia	96

Nigeria	98
A new country with a long history	98
A change in development: railways	100
Oil: benefits and problems	102
Using the oil wealth	104
Big projects	105
Towns and cities: Lagos	108

Nepal	110
Country of extremes	110
A country ready for change	112
Meeting basic needs	114
Tourism	116
Deforestation and soil erosion	118

Bangladesh	120
A country on a delta	120
Rich land, poor people	122
Reasons for poverty	124
Aid and development	125
What is development?	127

Index	128

Peru

2 Looking across the land of the Inca empire

Journey to Peru

The Spanish explorer Francisco Pizarro set out from Spain in January 1530 to conquer Peru. In December 1531, he sailed south from Panama and landed on the west coast of South America (1). The expedition force of 62 horsemen and 106 foot-soldiers took control of the coastal settlements and then moved into the mountains. The Inca empire, which had developed over many centuries, was soon to come to an end. The Incas allowed the Spaniards to march into the heart of their mountain empire (2). This was a terrible mistake. The small expedition, armed with swords, lances, crossbows and guns, massacred seven thousand Indians. By the end of 1533, Pizarro had control over the Inca capital of Cuzco and all the fabulous wealth of the Inca empire. Terraced mountain slopes (2), irrigation canals, huge stone buildings, a network of roads and stores of food to use in years when crops might fail, all show a civilization which had developed over thousands of years. The pattern of development was soon to change. The Spanish conquerors set the Indians to work on huge farm estates and in gold and silver mines. When the number of Indians dwindled because of hardship, European diseases and the breakdown of their traditional ways of living, the Spanish brought slaves from Africa to do the work.

Peru remained under Spanish rule for 300 years. The changes in society which happened then still affect the country today. Wealth and power are in the hands of a few people. These are mainly white people of Spanish descent. Business, industry and political power are centred in Lima, the capital city, which was founded by Pizarro in 1535. Ships still carry minerals, food, cotton and wool to Europe. The journey was made easier when the Panama canal opened in 1914 (3).

1 Pizarro's route to Peru

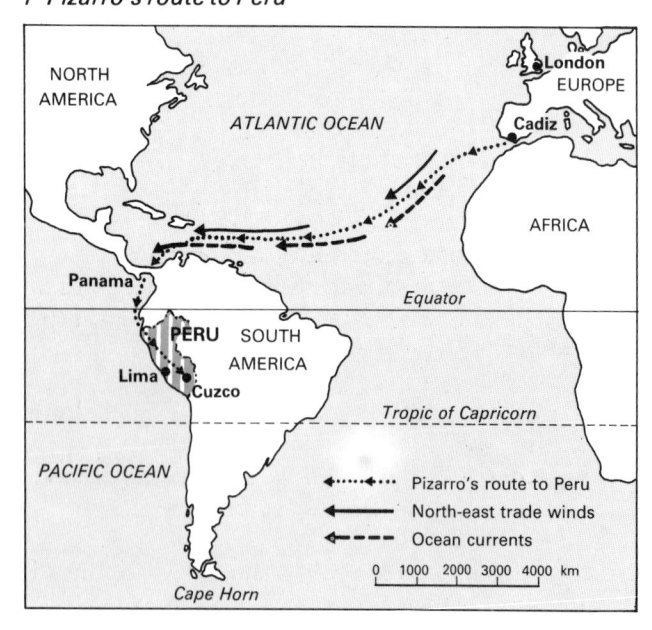

3 Using the Panama canal

Tourists and business people can fly direct to Lima from London. A plane leaves at 11.15 GMT and arrives at 20.50 local time. During their stay visitors will see remains of the Inca empire and perhaps compare Peru of the past with present-day Peru. They might think the Indians are poorer now than in the past, but they will also see that changes are taking place and new ideas about what 'development' really means are taking hold.

FOLLOW-UP WORK

1 What do you think the person meant who said
  (a) 'Peru is not as far away as it used to be';
  (b) 'Peru of the Inca empire was more developed than after 300 years of Spanish rule'?
2 Locate and compare the countries of the developing world that are included in this book. Ask for the map and statistics to use.

DEVELOPMENT

The changes which are needed to give everyone in the country a healthy and productive life.

DEVELOPING WORLD

All the countries where large changes are needed to give most people a healthy and productive life. Because most of these countries lie to the south of countries in Europe and North America, which are more developed, the term 'South' is often used to describe them.

The land of Peru

Peru is a large country, five times the size of the United Kingdom. Within its borders are three different areas of land we call regions. There is a narrow plain along the coast, called Costa, which is a desert. Mountains, called Sierra, rise steeply from the Costa to peaks over 6000 metres above sea level. Inland from the Sierra are lowlands which are covered with forest called Selva.

You can make a model which shows the three regions of Peru. Ask for the model sheet.

HOW TO PREPARE THE MODEL

(a) Colour the model lightly, using coloured pencils, like this:
Pacific Ocean, Lake Titicaca and rivers – blue
Coastal plain – yellow
Mountain slopes – brown
Trees of the interior forest – green
Towns and roads – red
(b) Stick the model onto thin card to make it stronger. Cut around the outline.
(c) Bend the centre section along the dashed lines to make angles which correspond to those on the side sections.
(d) (i) Cut along the dotted lines.
    (ii) Bend the flaps inwards at right angles along the dashed lines.
    (iii) Secure the flaps underneath the centre section with glue or adhesive tape.

Use your model for the study of the three regions of Peru on the next page.

THREE REGIONS OF PERU

4 Costa

5 Sierra

6 Selva

Temperatures

Peru lies between the Equator and latitude 18°S but only the Selva has tropical heat. Breezes from a cold current of water in the Pacific Ocean lower the temperatures in the Costa to between 20 °C and 25 °C. It also becomes colder as you climb into the mountains. Temperatures fall 6 degrees for every 1000 metres altitude.

1. Mark into the boxes on the side of the model the temperatures at 1000 metres, 2000 metres and 3000 metres above sea level.
2. Will there be snow on the mountain peaks? Give the reason for your answer.

Rainfall

3. Copy the cross-section (7). Colour the columns in blue to the correct height, using the rainfall statistics on the model.
4. The dry side of a mountain area is called the rainshadow area. Write the word 'rainshadow' onto the correct area of your cross-section.
5. Why do you think the south-east trade winds, shown on your model, bring heavy rain to the eastern slopes of the Sierra and light rainfall to the Costa?

7 Cross-section of Peru

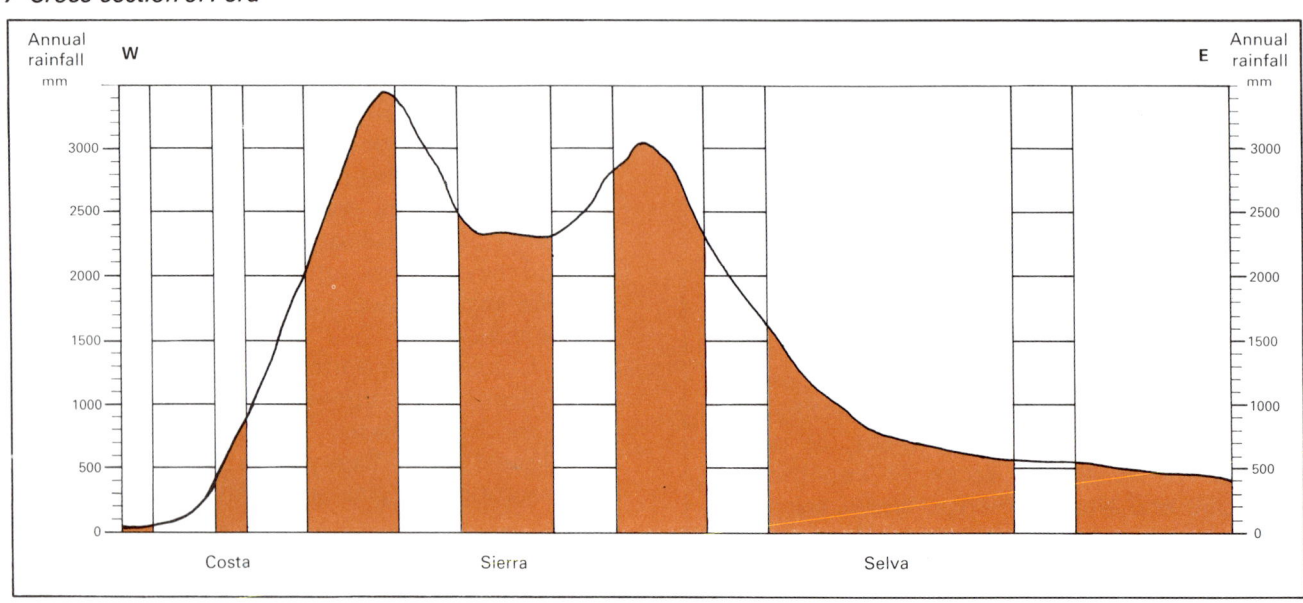

Farming

Eighty per cent of Peru is unsuitable for farming. There are steep rocky slopes in the Sierra, stony deserts in the Costa, and poor soils, covered with forest, in the Selva. Another 15 per cent of Peru is too cold to grow crops. These are the high mountain pastures which are used for grazing sheep and llamas. Only 5 per cent of the land can be used to grow crops. The best areas are near the rivers in the Costa, in sheltered valleys in the Sierra, and on patches of fertile soil in the Selva. The type of crops grown changes with the height of the land, and from one side of the mountains to the other.

6 Study the temperature and rainfall statistics on the model and the six sets of crops shown below. Select the set of crops you think belongs to each box, numbered from 1 to 6, on the model. Boxes 1 and 2 belong to the Costa, boxes 3 and 4 to the Sierra, and 5 and 6 to the Selva. Enter your crop choices onto the model.

A Rubber, oil palm, bananas
B Wheat, barley, potatoes
C Potatoes
D Coffee, tea, coca-shrubs
E Maize, oranges, beans
F Sugar cane, cotton, rice

LABOUR INTENSIVE

Work where the main input is from people rather than from machines.

Look at photo (8). How many men are working there? What would be the advantage and the problem of using machinery?

Transport and development

In the nineteenth century, railways were built to carry minerals from the mountains to the coast for export. In the twentieth century, roads are used to link the three regions of Peru. The Pan-American Highway runs the whole length of the coast, linking together all the main cities. Most roads in the mountains and forest are bumpy dirt tracks which turn to mud after heavy rain. New roads are needed.

7 What problems are there for rail transport in a mountain area?

8 (a) Oil and gas have been found in the Selva. A road is needed between Lima and the oil drilling site. Mark onto your model the route you would choose for this road.
  (b) A new road will link Matarani, Arequipa, Puno and Puerto Maldonado. Mark a route for this road onto your model.
  (c) There will be a *road network* when the two forest roads are linked by a road across the mountain slopes. Mark a route for this road onto your model.
  (d) What factors affected your choice of routes for the three roads you have marked?

9 (a) What is a road network?
  (b) Why will it take many years to build the road network?

10 How can roads help to develop the land of Peru?

8 Building a road in the mountains

A village in the Andes

Juliana Paxi is 10 years old. She lives in an Indian village on the plateau of southern Peru. Photograph (9) shows her carrying water from the river back to her home for drinking and cooking. Her 14-year-old brother, Pedro, and two younger sisters tag along. The water is dirty because it is used by a village upstream and animals excrete into it. Dirty water is the main reason why children get worms and diarrhoea. Malnutrition and dirty water are the main reasons why so many children in the village become sick or die.

A dusty track leads to the town of Puno over 50 kilometres away, but the Indians rarely go there. They live an isolated life and provide most of their own needs.

The houses are made from sun-dried brick called adobe, with a thatched roof. The living room is dark and unhealthy. When Mrs Paxi lights a fire with llama dung, the room fills with smoke and smell. The only light comes from the fire and an oil lamp. There is no toilet and the children defecate near the house.

Mrs Paxi and Juliana spend many hours spinning wool and weaving cloth to make blankets and ponchos. A poncho is a piece of cloth with a slit in the middle for the head to fit through.

When Mr Paxi married, he was given three small plots of land by his father. He grows potatoes, quinoa grain and cabbages. In September, he ploughs the stony soil with a wooden plough pulled by two oxen (10). If the summer rain comes in December, he can harvest enough food in June to feed his family. This is subsistence farming and he has nothing to sell. Sometimes the rain comes late and there may be a heavy frost at harvest-time. When this happens there is less food and the family goes hungry.

He grows the same crops each year on his one hectare of land. The llama dung he could use to improve the soil is burnt as fuel.

The two youngest girls are 4 and 5 years old. They look after the family's ten sheep, two llamas and two cattle. The children stay out on the cold windy plateau and there are no doctors to help them when they get ill. There is a school with one teacher but the children go there only if they are not needed to work in the fields or in the house.

9 Carrying water to the village

10 Ploughing the stony soils

ABSOLUTE POVERTY	MALNUTRITION
Lack of basic needs such as clean water, enough food, proper shelter, health care and education.	Illness caused by having only a little and poor food.
% of people living in poverty	Malnutrition in children %
Sierra 42	53
Costa 27	30
Selva 34	42

LAND REFORM

A change in the ownership of the land. Large landholdings are taken out of the hands of a few landowners and given to a large number of farmers.

Most Indian farmers live and work on small farms (minifundio). As the number of people has increased, the size of farms has decreased and become more fragmented. The best land has, for centuries, been divided into large estates called haciendas (latifundio) for commercial sheep and dairy farming. These farms were owned by landowners who often lived in the cities, but were worked by Indians for small wages or for their keep.

In the 1970s, the government took the haciendas from the landowners and gave them to the estate workers. Some land has been worked collectively and some divided into family plots. Farm output has fallen because the new owners cannot afford new seed and fertiliser and they are content to produce enough for the needs of the family rather than for the town markets. Most Indian farmers did not gain from the land reform because they did not work on the haciendas. The government has therefore tried to help them in other ways.

FOLLOW-UP WORK

1 What have been the advantages and problems of land reform?
2 The government has given money for six projects in the village (see below). There is a village committee to organise the projects. All the projects will be completed in three years.
    Select two projects you would start first. These are the projects you feel are needed most.
    Select two further projects for year 2 and the final projects for year 3. Give the reasons for the order you choose.
Nursery school. A team of men will build the school from concrete blocks and a tin roof. A local young man will be trained by the Ministry of Education to run a play school for children under 5 years old. Mothers will provide a meal for the children at the nursery school.
Clinic. The clinic will be built from concrete blocks and will have a tin roof. A local young man will be trained by the Ministry of Health. He will give vaccinations and sanitary help to children. He will advise parents on how to protect their children from parasites and disease.
Well. A shallow well will be dug by a team of men. The well will be lined with concrete and fitted with a hand pump. The well will provide clean water for the village (11).
Latrines. A team of men will dig pits for the disposal of excreta. Concrete squat areas will be covered with ventilated concrete-block shelters.

11 A new hand-pumped well

Children will be taught to use the latrines at nursery school.
Irrigation. A team of men will dig ditches to carry water from the river to the fields in the dry season.
Rotating fund. Ten families will be given money to buy seed, fertiliser and poultry. The money is given back when some of the crops and poultry are sold. The fund passes to ten different families each year.

3 Last year Mr Paxi worked for many months with a gang of men building a road across the mountains (8).
  (a) Why do you think he found this job necessary?
  (b) What problems might this have caused for the rest of the family?
  (c) Describe how he might spend the money he earned to improve life for his family in the village.
  (d) How might this new experience of work change his opinions about village life?

Moving out of the mountains

Mr Paxi decided to leave the village. He plans to follow the road he helped to build into the forest, to Pucallpa (12). Life will be very different in the forest. Pucallpa is a busy little town with 30 000 people living there. It is surrounded by thick forest. It is a five-day boat trip to Iquitos and it takes nine days to get back (12). The weather is always hot with temperatures between 30 °C and 38 °C. There is heavy rain most days and the air is very damp. Mr Paxi's lungs are adapted to breathing dry, thin air and he will find it very tiring working in the forest. The whole family will be pestered by insects and they are likely to catch tropical diseases. These are problems the family will have to overcome when Mr Paxi gets one of the following jobs in Pucallpa.

A *Road building.* A new road is being built across the eastern slopes of the mountains. This road will open up the forest area for development. Workers are needed on construction gangs.

B *Logging.* The best trees are cut and floated downstream to the sawmills in Pucallpa. There is a shortage of workers on the logging gangs.

C *Pulp and paper works.* There are jobs at the sawmill and pulp and paper works in Pucallpa.

D *Rice farming.* Forest has been cleared along the river and fertile alluvial soils are being farmed for rice. A few plots are available.

12 Departments of Peru: where people live

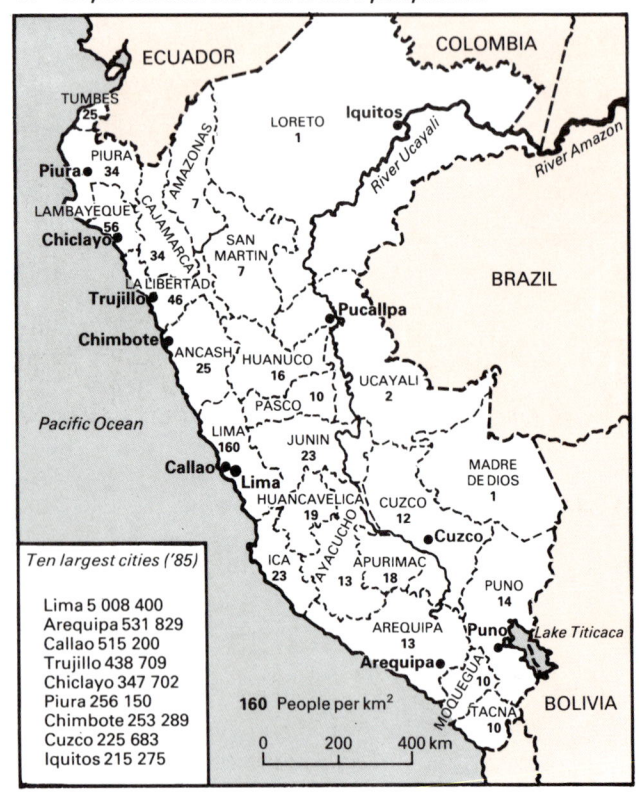

Road building in the forest

E *Oil exploration.* Oil and gas discoveries near Pucallpa have led to more exploration by international oil companies. Men are needed to clear the forest and help the survey teams.

The statistics in table (13) show that most people have moved to the coast rather than into the forest.

13 Population of Peru (1941–86)

Year	Population (millions)	Where they live		
		Costa	Sierra	Selva
1941	6	30%	65%	5%
1961	10	39%	52%	9%
1981	18	50%	40%	10%
1986	20	60%	32%	8%

FOLLOW-UP WORK

1 Which job in the forest region do you think will be most suitable for Mr Paxi? Give your reasons.

2 (a) Draw pie-graphs (divided circles) to show where people lived in 1941 and 1986. Use table (13). Colour the Costa segment yellow, the Sierra segment brown and the Selva segment green.
  (b) What changes have occurred in where people live in Peru?

3 On your own copy of map (12) colour each department using the following code:

Population density	Colour
0– 9	green
10–29	brown
30–59	orange
60 and over	red

Describe the pattern of population density shown on your map. Suggest some reasons for the differences.

Lima

Lima was founded by Francisco Pizarro on the banks of the river Rimac (14). The river was one of the few which flowed across the desert from the Andes mountains to the Pacific Ocean. The Rimac had provided water for drinking and irrigation for many hundreds of years before the Spaniards arrived. The valley leads upstream to mines in the mountains and downstream to the sheltered port of Callao. This was a perfect site and location for a city which would be the administration centre for the Spanish empire in South America and outlet for Peru's wealth in raw materials.

The ruling elite concentrated power in Lima. Roads and later railways focused here. Cathedrals, churches and universities secured its position as the religious and educational centre. Industries were set up to process raw materials and feed and clothe the growing population. More recent additions include engineering and car assembly. When the large landowners lost their estates in the 1970s they invested the money they received in compensation in business and industry in Lima. As you can see, the process of concentrating power and development in Lima has continued through the centuries with much less development in other parts of the country. As a result, Lima has grown larger than all the other towns and has a big proportion of the country's business, industry and services (12, 15). It is a primate city.

PRIMATE CITY

A city which dominates all other cities in the country. There is a large gap between the size of its population and the second ranking city.

---

15 *Growth of population in Lima and Peru, and industry and services in Lima/Callao*

Growth of population (millions)			Percentage of Peru's business industry and services in Lima/Callao	
	Peru	Lima		
1940	6	0.5	Manufacturing industry	68
1950	8	1.0	All full-time jobs	40
1960	10	1.7	Earnings from	
1970	14	3.1	business/trade	60
1980	18	4.6	Imports to Peru	65
1985	20	5.0	Exports from Peru	40
			Private investment	98
			Hospital beds	50

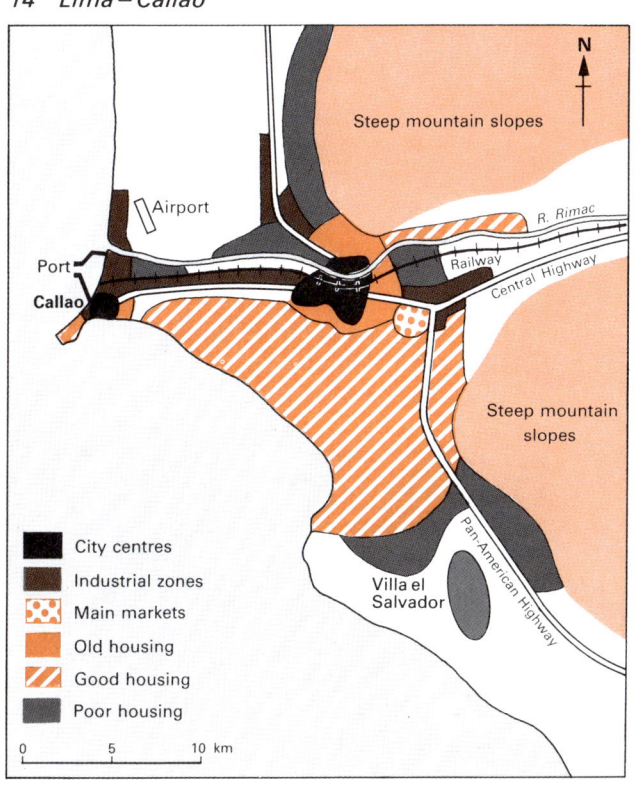

14 *Lima – Callao*

16 *The centre of Lima*

FOLLOW-UP WORK

1. What proportion of the people in Peru lived in Lima in (a) 1940 and (b) 1985?
2. How many times larger is Lima than the second ranking city, Arequipa?
3. What advantages and problems might there be for concentrating political, industrial and business power in one place for (a) Lima and (b) other towns in Peru?

In the centre of Lima there is the Presidential Palace, Cathedral, City Hall, modern shops, restaurants and entertainments. In photograph (16) notice the tower blocks of offices, hotels and apartments. Map (14) shows that industry has spread along the roads, railway and port. There are widespreading suburbs with modern houses, tree-lined streets, parks and shopping centres. It is not surprising that the city has attracted students and business and professional people from all parts of Peru.

Hundreds of poor people also arrive in Lima every week. They come mainly from the Sierra. There are *push* and *pull* factors at work (see below). When you have also read about the Perez family on page 13, do the exercises.

FOLLOW-UP WORK

1 Compare the life of the Paxi family in the Sierra with that of the Perez family in Lima. Use the following headings:
   Water   Fuel   House   Work
   Education   Health   Local environment

2 Use your comparison of the two families to decide whether the main reasons for people moving from the Sierra to Lima are *push* factors, *pull* factors or both *push and pull* factors.

3 Lima has grown large because of young immigrants from the Sierra and a large natural increase in population. What link can you see between these two factors? What effect will this have on the villages in the Sierra?

4 Draw a line graph to show the growth of population in Lima from 1940 to 1985. Describe changes in the rate of growth shown on your graph.

5 Study map (14).
   (a) Why are shops, offices and hotels located at the centre of the city?
   (b) Why are the oldest houses near the centre of the city?
   (c) Why are factories located along the roads and at the coast?
   (d) Why do poor people live on steep slopes at the edge of the city?
   (e) Why have Lima and Callao become one city?

6 Locate the world's fastest growing cities. Ask for the map and statistics to use.

PUSH FACTORS

These are the reasons people leave rural (countryside) areas.

1 Small farms provide little food. Land divided amongst sons makes smaller fragmented farms.
2 Hard manual work. Subsistence. No money for seed, fertiliser, fuel, schooling.
3 Husbands often seek seasonal jobs leaving family to cope on own.
4 Boring life in long cold winter.
5 Hardship when crops lost in frost, flood or drought.
6 Isolated farms. No contact with other people.
7 Poor housing. No electricity, sanitation or clean water. Short of fuel for heating and cooking.
8 Sickness, malnutrition and rotting teeth. No health care. Constant suffering.
9 Little schooling. Children look after animals all day.

PULL FACTORS

These are the reasons people are attracted to urban (town and city) areas.

1 Jobs in factories, commerce and services.
2 Money earning to buy variety of food and drink. Local market for own craft work.
3 Work for both husbands and wives.
4 Shops and entertainments.
5 Help from urban councils. Community activities.
6 Transport. Buses.
7 Houses with access to piped water, sanitation and electricity.
8 Clinics and hospitals.
9 Schools, books, pens and paper.

Living in a shanty town

Carlos Perez is 12 years old. He lives in a shanty town on the desert hills in the south of Lima. The photograph (17) shows him collecting water from an old oil drum. The family buys four drums of water each week from a tanker-lorry. After a few days in the sun, the water is unfit to drink. It must be boiled before it is used.

Carlos was 2 years old when he came to Lima. His father was a farmer in the Sierra and he sold his land and rented a flat in the old part of the city. Lima with its modern buildings (16) seemed full of opportunity. One hundred thousand people arrived in the city in the same year as the Perez family, all of them looking for work. After a few months without a job Mr Perez had to leave the flat. He built a house from matting like the one in the photograph (18). This was on the hillside at the edge of the city.

Mr Perez' first job was a street seller. He made a small profit selling cheap shirts and socks. Later he found work in a clothing factory and his wife has an office-cleaning job. They have built a new house with concrete blocks and a corrugated-iron roof. The shanty town now has electricity and the family has electric light and television. Carlos goes to school where he has learnt Spanish. He is a healthy boy and rarely has to visit the local doctor or clinic.

17 Collecting water from a drum

18 A house made from matting

SHANTY TOWN

An area of houses which poor people have built for themselves from whatever materials are available to them. The settlement is on the outskirts of the city. In Lima they are called barriadas but the authorities call them 'pueblos jovenes' (young towns).

Almost a third of the 5 million people of Lima live in shanty towns. These spread up the barren hillsides (19) and across the desert plains at the southern edge of the city. The contrast between rich and poor in Lima is as clear as the contrast between Lima (the core) and the rest of Peru (the periphery) (20).

In 1971 the city authorities, faced with thousands of squatters on land near the city centre, gave them land 25 kilometres further south. Here they laid out a grid of streets and plots of land where the poor people, mainly Indians from the Sierra, could build houses for themselves in the desert. Twenty-five years later the shanty town had grown into a city of 300 000 people called Villa el Salvador (14).

There are no jobs and most men make the hour-long bus ride into Lima six days a week. Thirty per cent have jobs in the city but the rest are looking for work or are part of the army of 90 000 hawkers in the streets. This is the 'informal sector' of employment which is the biggest employer in most cities in the developing world.

Everyone in Villa el Salvador is poor. Most people do not have enough to eat and infant mortality is high.

The plight of poor people in cities in both the developed and the developing world is bad, but without social security and with lack of resources the problems of developing countries are extreme. In Villa el Salvador people try to improve life by

19 Hillside shanty town

community effort. People are organised in neighbourhoods, 24 houses to a block and 16 blocks in a neighbourhood. Each neighbourhood has a committee and they set up kitchens which have also become centres for health care, schooling and small money-making enterprises. Most of this work is done by women. The committees need money and hope for help from the Lima city authorities and from international aid organisations.

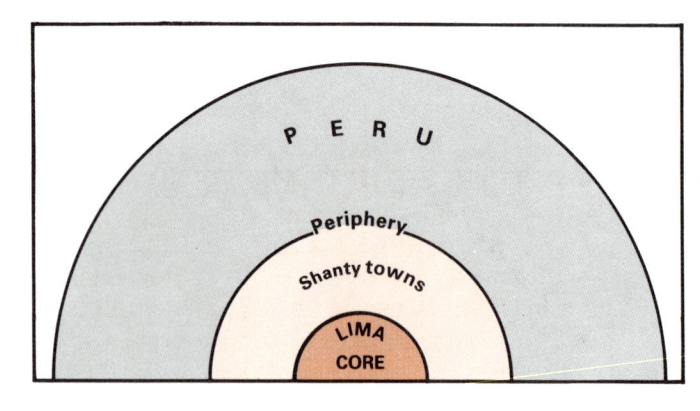

FOLLOW-UP WORK

1 Imagine that you are a member of a committee in Villa el Salvador during the early years of its growth. In what order of importance (rank order) would you place these development plans: Clinics Electricity Factory jobs Farms Hospitals Parks Paved roads Refuse collection Street lighting Sewage disposal Schools Supermarkets Train service to Lima
2 Give reasons for the order you choose.

TOPIC FOR DISCUSSION

One way to help solve the problems of poverty in Lima and the rest of Peru would be to spread wealth and development more evenly from the core to the periphery; from the city to the shanty towns and from the Lima region to the other regions of Peru (20, 12).

20 Core and periphery

Irrigating the desert

The coastal plain of Peru is a desert (4). This is one of the driest places in the world. South-east trade winds bring rain to the eastern slopes of the Andes mountains, but they are dry winds when they reach the coastal plains. The coast is in the rainshadow of the mountains as was shown on the model, page 6.

There is a cold current of water near the coast called the Peruvian current. Air passing over the current is cool when it reaches land. Although the air comes off the sea, it does not bring rain. The cool air warms as it goes over the land and evaporates moisture from the ground.

Hundreds of rivers flow down the western slopes of the mountains towards the desert. They are fed by melting snow and rain from the high Andes in summer. Only 52 rivers reach the Pacific Ocean. The others peter out in the desert.

Rivers provide irrigation water to grow crops. There are the remains of irrigation canals and fields on the north coast of Peru which date back more than a thousand years. The Spaniards, as early as the seventeenth century, set up large cotton and sugar plantations using irrigation. Photograph (21) shows fields of irrigated crops near Lima in the 1980s. Three crops are grown every year in the constant heat of the desert. In 1975 the government decided to begin work on the largest irrigation project in South America. It is called the Majes project. The area is shown on map (22) and details of the scheme are on page 16.

22 *Location of the Majes project*

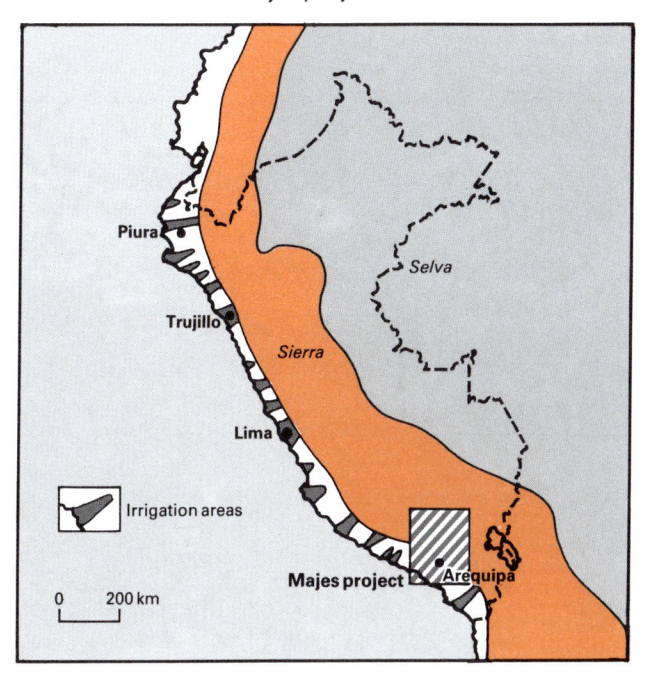

21 *Irrigated land near Lima*

IRRIGATION

The artificial distribution of water to the land to make possible or improve the growth of crops in areas of low or seasonal rainfall. Water can be taken from rivers which cross dry areas or transferred from water surplus areas to water deficit areas. Seasonal rain can be stored behind dams and used when it is needed.

Irrigation increases crop yields (see below), provides water at the optimum times and allows more than one crop to be grown in a year. The main problems are the cost and build-up of salt in the soil.

Crop yields with or without irrigation (kg per hectare)

	Costa	Sierra	Selva
Potatoes			
Rainfed	–	5900	–
Irrigated	14000	7900	–
Wheat			
Rainfed	–	900	–
Irrigated	2000	1100	–
Maize			
Rainfed	–	900	1600
Irrigated	3450	1450	2200
Rice			
Rainfed	–	–	1700
Irrigated	5000	4500	4700

FOLLOW-UP WORK

1 What advantages will the Majes project have for Peru?
2 Suggest reasons why many small irrigation schemes in the Costa, Sierra and Selva might have been better than one big project. Consider cost, debt, employment, time to complete, the spread of development. Study the statistics above and the information on page 16.

23 The Majes project

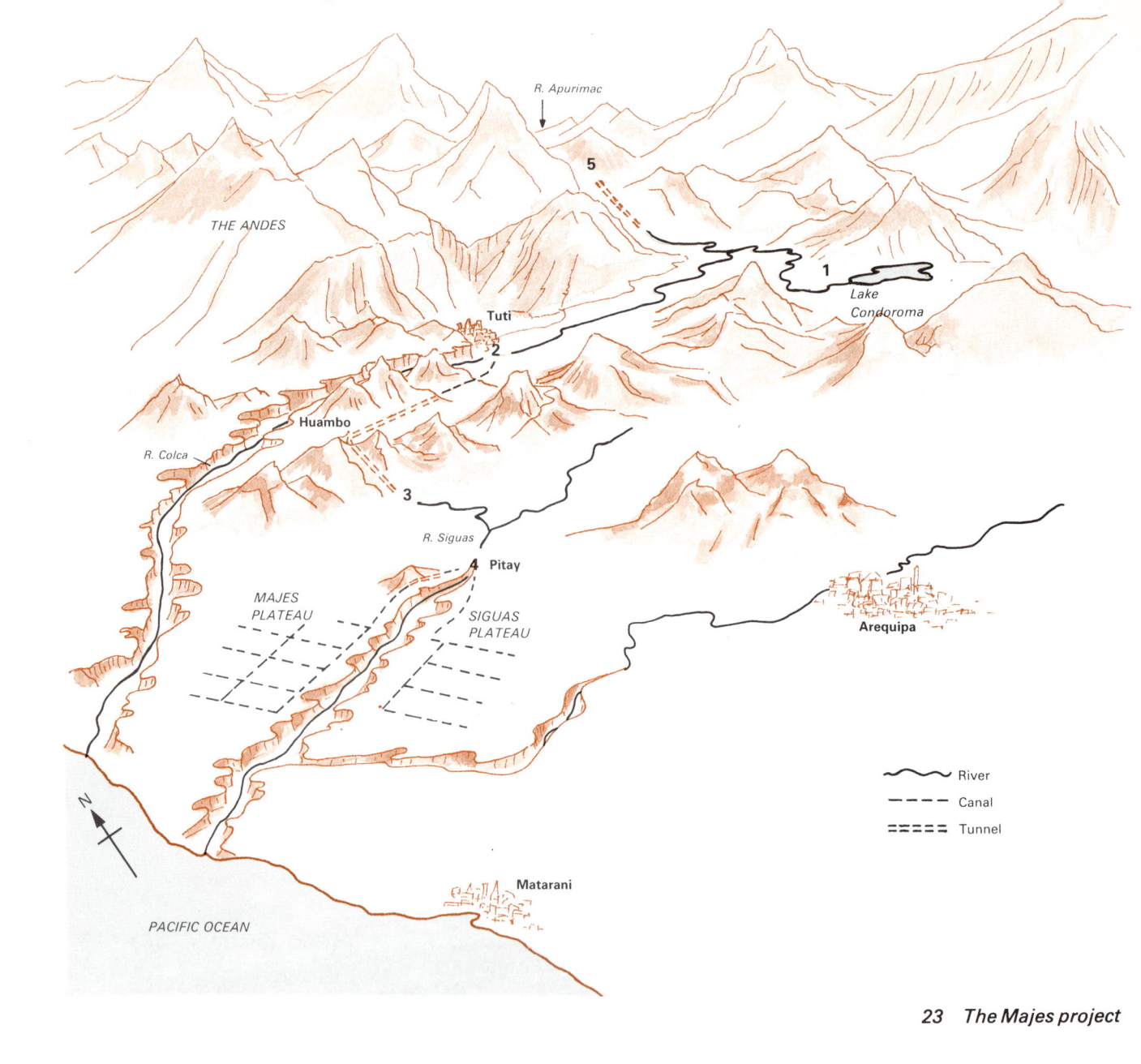

	DETAILS OF THE MAJES PROJECT
Cost	One billion pounds. Half from foreign loans with interest to pay. Half from government funds raised from taxes. The amount accounts for 60% of money spent on agriculture each year.
Method	Capital-intensive, using machinery and high technology. Foreign supervisors, engineers and equipment. A few hundred jobs for Indians.
Area	600 square kilometres of the Majes plateau and Siguas plateau will be irrigated.
Progress	Stage 1 which provides one-third of the water supply was completed in 1985. This includes the Condoroma dam (1) and water transfer from the river Colca (2) via tunnels to the river Siguas (3) with ditches and canals to the desert plains from Pitay (4). Hydro-electric power stations at sites 3 and 4. Stage 2 to begin. Drilling through the Andes (5) to capture water from the river Apurimac which flows to the Amazon.
Use	Farmland for 50 000 people when complete. Irrigated land for grain, fruit, vegetables, meat and milk. Hydro-electric power for new industries in Arequipa.
Problems	Earthquake-prone area. Cost per hectare four times that of small schemes.

Selling the country's resources

Peru, like most developing countries, provides the raw materials which are used by industrial countries in the North. This is a pattern which was developed in colonial times and which has continued to the present day. The money earned from these exports is used to buy food, machinery and equipment and to pay for new roads and the Majes project, for example. Countries in the developed world can make a big profit selling goods manufactured from Peru's resources (24).

24 Exports

Main products exported from Peru (1985)	% of total exports (by value)	Main uses for these exports	Main markets for all these products (%)	
Petroleum	22	Petrol, chemicals	USA	36
Copper	16	Electric wire, piping, coins	Japan	10
Zinc	9	Galvanisation, pharmaceuticals, paint	USSR	5
Textiles	8	Clothing	West Germany	5
Lead	7	Batteries, solder, ammunition	UK	5
Silver	5	Coins, photography, electronics	Korea	3
Coffee	5	Drink	Belgium	3
Fish	4	Fertiliser, animal feed	Italy	3
Iron ore	3	Steel	Others	30
Cotton	2	Clothing		
Others	19	Other minerals, sugar and wool		

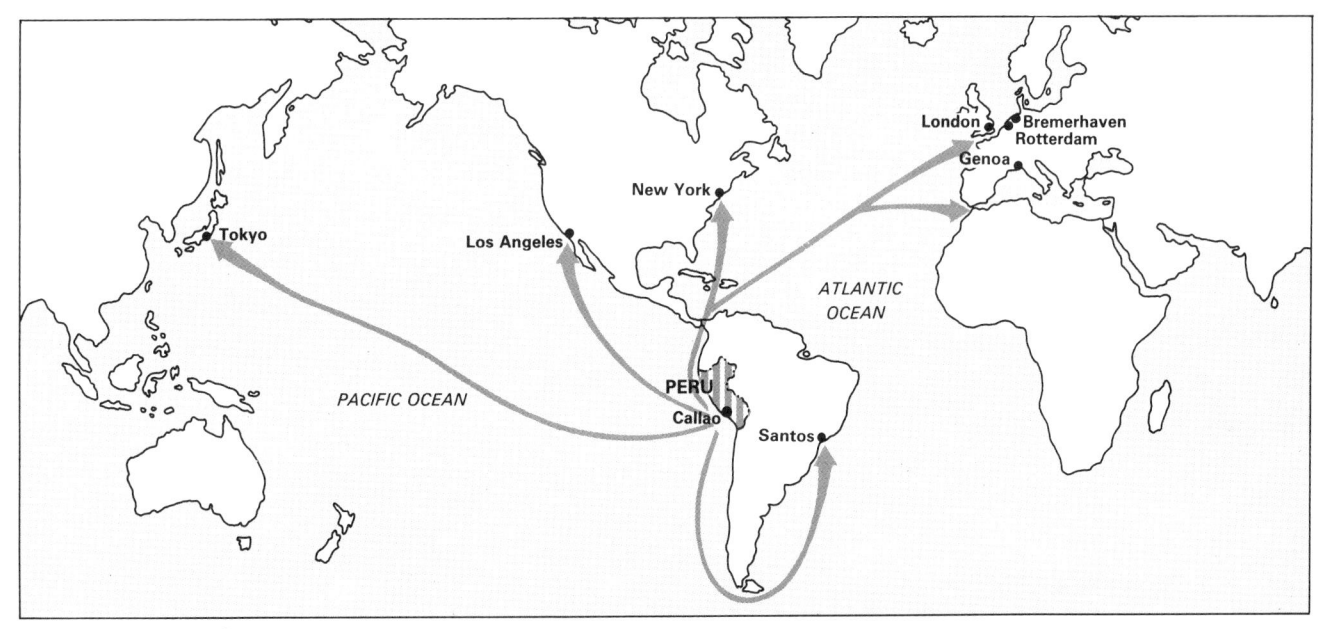

25 Routes to markets

FOLLOW-UP WORK

1 Study chart (24) of Peruvian exports.
  (a) How can you tell that Peru is not an industrial country?
  (b) Why do the USA and Japan buy large amounts of products from Peru?
  (c) Why is Peru fortunate in having many products to sell rather than one main product?
  (d) In 1988, Peru's reserves of oil were expected to last seven more years. What problems will Peru face if the oil runs out in 1995?
  (e) How might Peru benefit by reducing imports of manufactured goods and increasing home manufacturing industries?

2 Study map (25) of routes to markets.
  (a) Make a list of the main ports shown on the map. Name the country to which each belongs.
  (b) Why has Peru a good location for the export of raw materials?
  (c) Why do ships take a southern route to Santos?
  (d) Why is it easier to reach west coast USA than east coast USA?
  (e) Is it a shorter route to London or to Tokyo?

Industrial fishing

The cool waters of the Peruvian current are rich in fish. Shoals of anchovies feed at or near to the surface of the sea. Sea birds eat a million tonnes of these fish every year, but the Peruvians catch more.

Fish that live near the surface of the sea are called pelagic fish and they are caught in purse seine nets. Men in a small boat hold one end of the net which is paid out from the seiner. As the seiner circles a shoal, the net hangs down from the surface like a curtain (26,27). When a line is pulled tight through metal rings at the bottom of the net, the fish are trapped in the purse. The net is winched on deck and the catch is drawn to the side of the ship. The fish are pumped on board through a pipe and the ship returns to port.

Only ten per cent of the catch is used as food. Ninety per cent of fish are taken to factories where the oil is removed and the flesh dried in rotary driers (28). The dried fish are ground to flour called fishmeal. Fishmeal is rich in protein and minerals and is exported to the USA and Europe to feed cattle, pigs and poultry.

In 1970, Peru took the largest catch of fish in the world. Over 12 million tonnes of fish were landed by over 1500 purse seiners. This catch was converted into 2 million tonnes of fishmeal and 300 000 tonnes of fish oil at 99 factories along the coast of Peru.

Graph (29) shows the rapid growth of the fishing industry until 1970.

28 *Fish processing works*

26 *Purse seiner fishing boat*

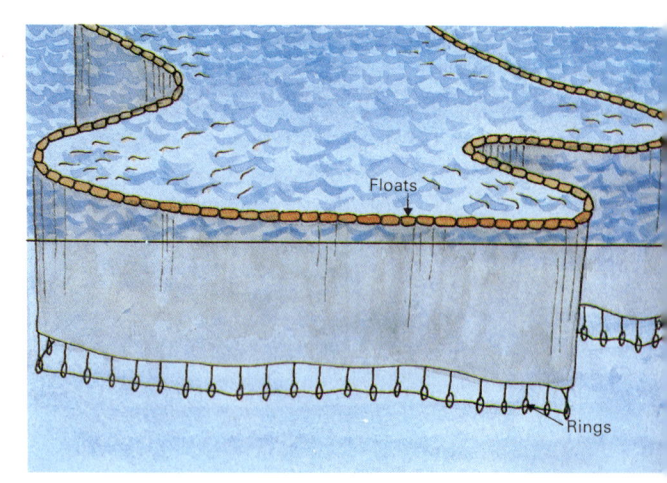

27 *Parts of a purse seine net*

29 *Growth of fishing*

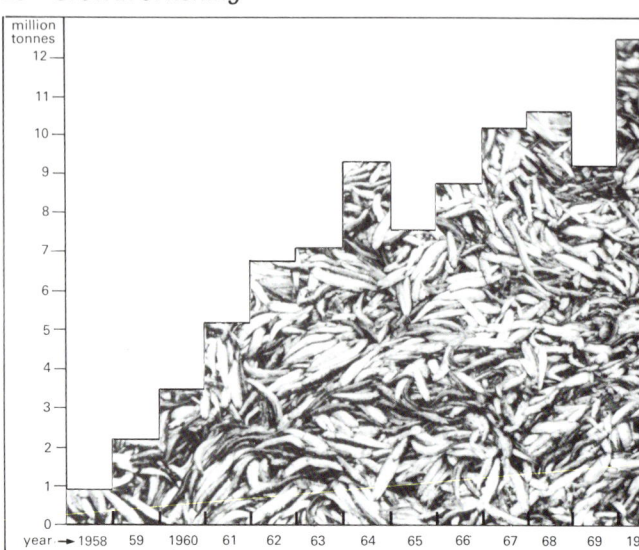

Crisis

In 1972, disaster struck the fishing industry in Peru. The anchovy shoals disappeared from coastal waters. There were two reasons for this happening: the 'El Nino' current (30) and overfishing (31).

Anchovies thrive in cool water. In 1972, a current of warm water entered the fishing grounds from the Equator. The current is called 'El Nino' (The Child) because it has visited Peru in the past at Christmas. Millions of anchovies died and the remaining shoals moved to cool waters off the coast of Chile and far out into the Pacific Ocean.

Although cool waters returned to the coast of Peru, there were fewer anchovies than in the past.

30 The 'El Nino' current (December 1982)

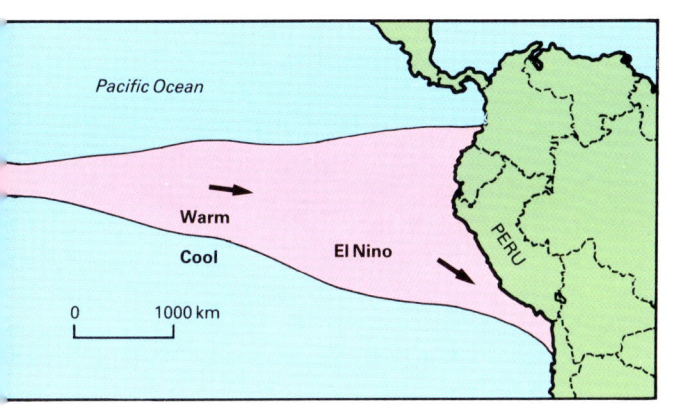

31 Overfishing

The reason was that Peru had fished anchovies faster than they were breeding. As the production of fishmeal became greater, the stocks of fish in the sea became smaller. In 1982, 'El Nino' returned (30) and stayed for a year. The effect on Peru's fishing is shown on the graph (32).

32 Decline of fishing

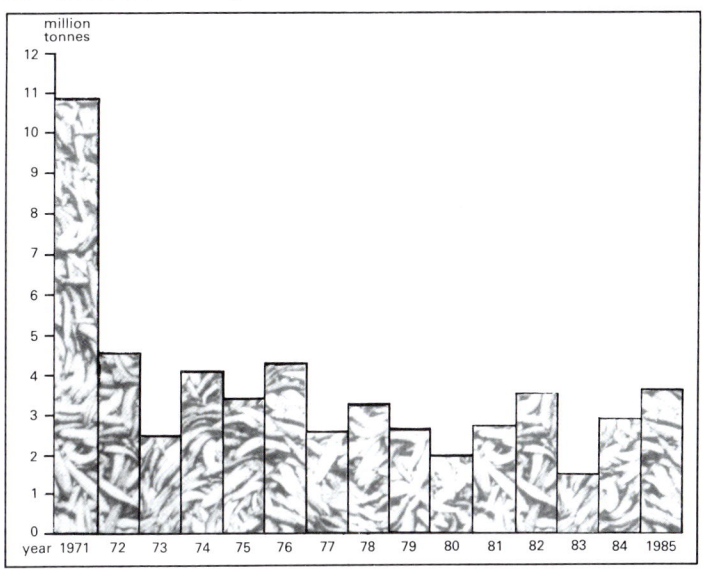

FOLLOW-UP WORK

1 In 1973, the government took control of the fishing industry. The aim was to conserve stocks of fish in the sea and safeguard the jobs of half a million people in the fishing industry. Copy the following sentences into your book. Complete them by adding either 'reduced' or 'increased'. Briefly say how your decisions would help the government achieve its aim.
   (a) The number of purse seiners must be _____.
   (b) The number of fishmeal factories must be _____.
   (c) The number of anchovies caught must be _____.
   (d) The number of other types of fish caught will be _____.
   (e) The amount of fish used as food should be _____.
   (f) The price paid for the fish landed at port should be _____.
   (g) Fish breeding projects should be _____.

2 (a) What lessons can Peru learn from the fishing industry disaster?
   (b) How might this disaster influence Peru in her future development of:
      (i) *forests* for making pulp and paper;
      (ii) *oil* for making energy and chemicals?

Minerals from the mountains

Peru has been a mining country for centuries. The Incas mined large amounts of gold, silver and copper and they made alloys such as bronze. Modern mining began with the development of the great copper deposits of Cerro de Pasco. The railway reached there in 1895 and a large smelter was built nearby in 1919 (33). The region around Arequipa is also rich in metallic minerals; the railway reached these mines in 1870.

Ores are mined at the surface in open pits and from underground mines. An ore is a rock which contains a useful amount of metal. The copper ores have 2 per cent copper content and the rock has to be crushed and smelted to remove the metal from the waste. The ores occur in veins which the miners call lodes. These are cracks in the rock which are filled with the valuable ores. Hot gases and fluids, from deep in the Earth, found their way to the surface along cracks in the rock. When the fluids cooled, the ores were formed. Peru is rich in metallic minerals and only 12 per cent of the veins have been mined.

33 Copper smelter in the Andes

FOLLOW-UP WORK

Study sketch (34) which shows what a mining scene might look like if all the parts were visible at the same time.

1 Copy the following passage into your book. Choose a suitable word for each blank space after studying the correct lettered area of the sketch of mining in the Andes.

Ores are mined at the surface using __A__ and underground using __B__. The ores are carried to the smelter by __C__ and by __D__. Power for the smelters comes from the __E__. Smoke from the copper smelter and refinery is released into the air through a __F__. Poisonous fumes from the zinc smelter are released into the high atmosphere through a __G__ which has been laid on the steep mountain slopes.

The workers and their family live at the mine in either terraced __H__ or in blocks of __I__. There is a hospital, community centre, clinic and a very modern __J__. The mine and settlement are linked to the coast by __K__ and __L__.

2 Write about the effects that mining has had upon the environment of the Andes. Draw your own sketch, with labels added to it, to accompany your writing.
3 What problems will there be mining 4000 metres up in the mountains?
4 Why are the smelters located at the mine rather than on the coast where the metals are exported?
5 In what ways is life better for mining families than for families living in villages in the Andes?
6 Suggest two ways in which the mining of Peru's resources benefits other countries more than Peru.
7 In recent years the costs of mining have risen but world prices for minerals have fallen. What problems will this bring to Peru?
8 Suggest advantages and problems of capital-intensive methods for mining.

CAPITAL INTENSIVE

Work where the main input is from expensive machinery and equipment rather than from people. Mining provides less than 2% of jobs in Peru but more than 40% of export earnings.

Foreign companies own 60% of the mines. The largest is the US-owned Southern Peru Copper Corporation. They provide the money (capital) and technology and take much of the profit.

---

34 Mining scene in the Andes ▶

21

Links across the continent

Peru, Colombia, Bolivia, Venezuela and Ecuador form the 'common market' of the Andes (35). Their aim is to help each other in their plans for development and provide a better life for all the people in the five countries.

New roads have been built between them (36) and they trade freely with each other.

They plan their farming and industry together. One example is the motor vehicle industry. The five countries need about half a million vehicles each year. Each country makes one size of car or type of truck which is sold to the whole market. Parts are made in each country and assembled in large factories built by big motor vehicle companies from the USA, Europe and Japan.

Table (37) shows some details of each country in 1986.

35 The Andes common market

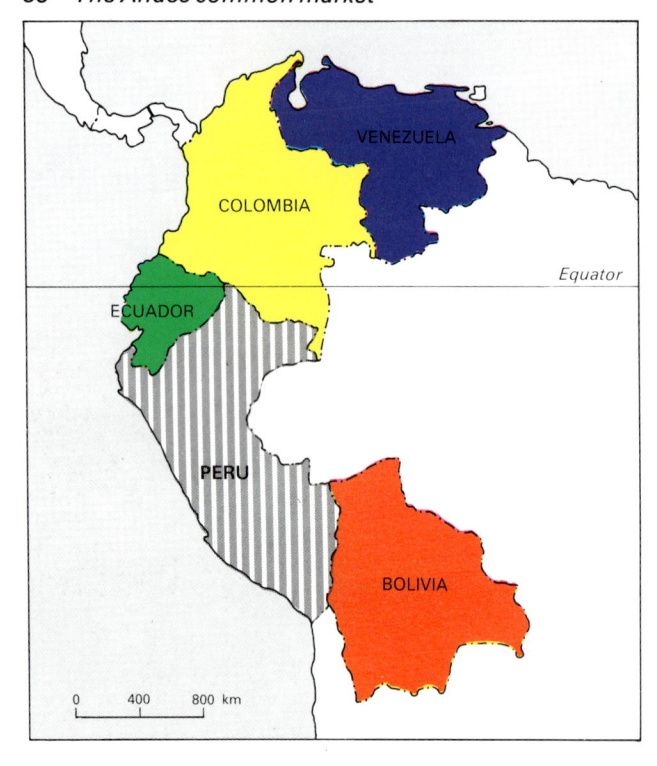

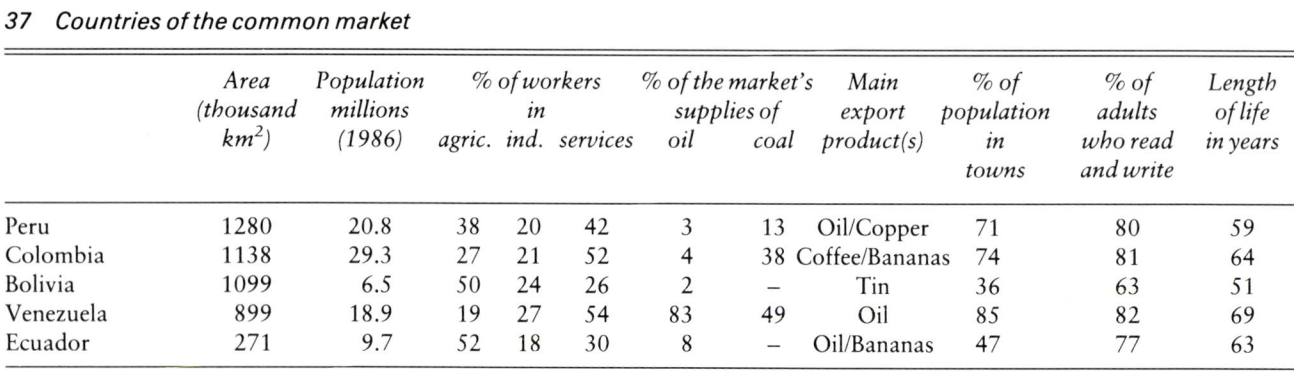

36 Road across the Andes

FOLLOW-UP WORK

Use map (35) and table (37) to help you answer the following questions
1. (a) Which is the poorest country in the Andes common market?
   (b) How can other countries of the common market help this poor country?
2. What advantages are there in five countries joining together to make motor vehicles?
3. The common market has plans to develop the steel industry. Should they build one large steelworks or a small steelworks in each country? Give your reasons.
4. Why do you think there is little trade between these countries in:
   (a) farm products;
   (b) oil and minerals?

PAN-AMERICAN HIGHWAY GAME

Each player builds highways which link all the countries of South America. There are mountains to cross, forests to penetrate and resources to develop. Ask for further details.

37 Countries of the common market

	Area (thousand km^2)	Population millions (1986)	% of workers in agric.	% of workers in ind.	% of workers in services	% of the market's supplies of oil	% of the market's supplies of coal	Main export product(s)	% of population in towns	% of adults who read and write	Length of life in years
Peru	1280	20.8	38	20	42	3	13	Oil/Copper	71	80	59
Colombia	1138	29.3	27	21	52	4	38	Coffee/Bananas	74	81	64
Bolivia	1099	6.5	50	24	26	2	–	Tin	36	63	51
Venezuela	899	18.9	19	27	54	83	49	Oil	85	82	69
Ecuador	271	9.7	52	18	30	8	–	Oil/Bananas	47	77	63

Brazil

One-half of South America

Brazil is the fifth largest country in the world after the USSR, Canada, China and the USA. Within the borders of the country lies half the land area of South America. This is a country of contrasts. In the north-west is tropical rainforest, called selva. In the north-east is a dry area of thorn bushes and trees, called caatinga (1). Most of the land is plateau and plain and there are good opportunities for farming, mining and industry. But the great size of the country also brings problems. Most people live near the east coast in cities such as Sao Paulo and Rio de Janeiro. Roads have to be built thousands of kilometres into the interior to make the land accessible and useful.

There were 280 million people in South America in 1987 and half lived in Brazil. This is the sixth largest population in the world after China, India, USSR, USA and Indonesia. There are great contrasts in the lives of the people. These contrasts are clearly seen in Rio de Janeiro (2). Millions of tourists visit the city every year. They see modern blocks of flats and offices, new factories, a busy port and airport, wide roads and one of the longest bridges in the world across the bay. Of the six million people who live in Rio, one-quarter live in the shanty towns, called favelas, which cover the hillsides around the city (3). Although Brazil is quickly becoming a modern industrial country, a large number of people live in poverty.

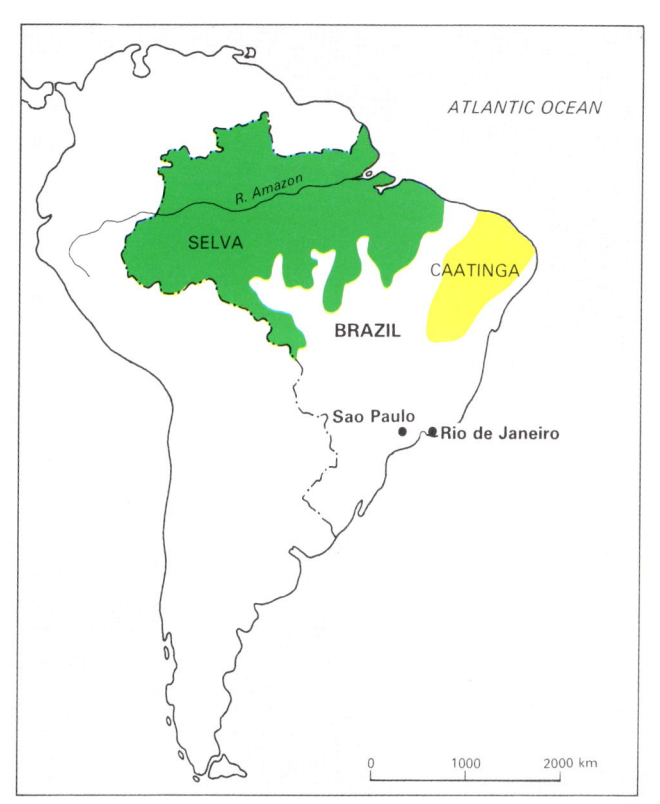

1 Brazil

2 Rio de Janeiro

3 A favela

FOLLOW-UP WORK

1. The area of Brazil is 8 512 000 km² (square kilometres) and the UK is 245 000 km². How many times larger than the UK is Brazil?
2. Use the scale on map (1) to measure the distance across Brazil (a) north to south, (b) east to west.
3. Draw a sketch based on the two photographs. Use the title 'The two faces of Rio de Janeiro'. Write about the contrasts shown in your sketch.

Poverty in the dry north-east

Thirty per cent of all Brazilians live in north-east Brazil. This is the poorest part of the country with most people scratching a living from the land (4). One-fifth of all families are hungry. They do not have enough food to give them the energy to do a full day's work. Hungry people become sick and disabled and they die at an early age. The statistics in table (5) show a great contrast between conditions of life in north-east and south-east Brazil, where there are modern industries and large cities.

5 Comparing north-east and south-east Brazil

	North-east Brazil	South-east Brazil
Average length of life	48 years	63 years
Babies dying before the age of 1 year	19%	7%
Houses with clean water to drink	20%	78%
Houses with sewage disposal	25%	73%
Children aged 10 to 14 attending school	57%	83%

You have to look back more than 300 years to find some of the reasons why people live in poverty today. When the Portuguese landed on the north-east coast in 1500, they found a land occupied by Indians. Unlike the Incas of Peru, these Indians lived a simple life and they had no gold or silver to plunder. The first European settlements were trading posts on the coast. The Indians supplied logs of Brazilwood in exchange for axes and trinkets. The wood has a red dye which was used in Europe for dyeing cloth. In the 1530s, the Portuguese planted sugar cane on the coastal plain. Negro slaves were brought from Africa to do the work.

From these beginnings came Brazil's mixed population of Indians, Portuguese and Negroes. The large sugar plantations are still located on the coast (6). Further inland, there are more large estates with cotton, maize and beef cattle. These large farms are called latifundia. They are owned by a few wealthy businessmen who often live far away in Sao Paulo and Rio de Janeiro. The poor peasants live in the dry interior on small plots of land called minifundia or they work for very low wages on the latifundia.

4 Collecting wood from the caatinga

6 Loading sugar cane

One reason for the poverty of peasant farmers in north-east Brazil is the lack of rain. There is a dry season from May to November with temperatures rising to 37 °C. South-east trade winds from the Atlantic Ocean bring rain in the summer months (7). In some years the winds are weak and the interior has a drought. When the wells dry up, the water-seller is a familiar sight as he brings drinking water to small inland towns (8). But without rain the crops die and families go hungry or pack their belongings and move into the cities.

The river Sao Francisco flows 2900 kilometres across the centre of Brazil before finding its way to the sea halfway between Salvador and Recife. There are fertile silt soils near to the river banks where farmers grow rice, maize, beans and manioc. Three large dams have been built across the river (7) to store the water and to generate electricity. But these modern developments do not help poor farmers. The reservoirs cover the best soils, the electricity is used in coastal cities, and irrigation water goes to the cane fields (9) and other latifundia.

7 *Rainfall, population and agriculture*

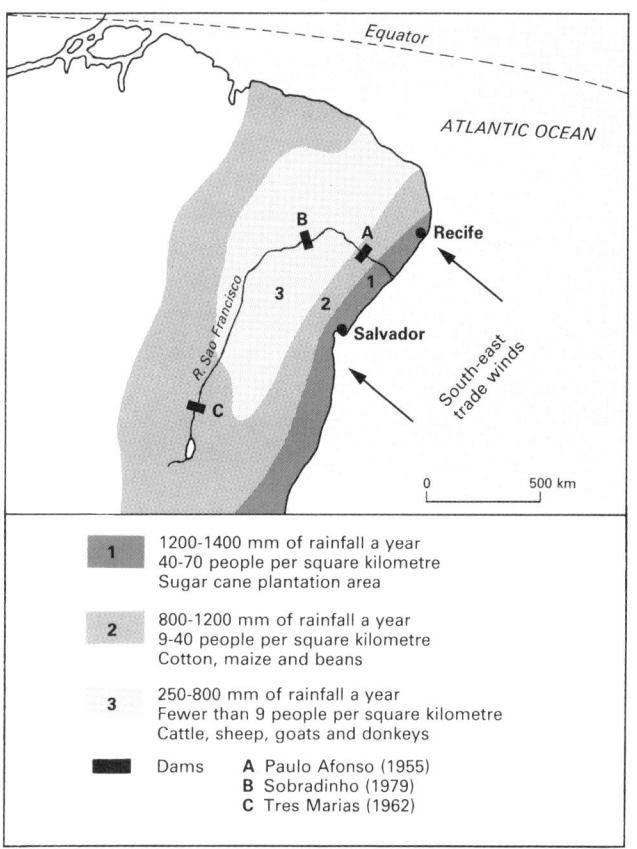

1	1200-1400 mm of rainfall a year 40-70 people per square kilometre Sugar cane plantation area
2	800-1200 mm of rainfall a year 9-40 people per square kilometre Cotton, maize and beans
3	250-800 mm of rainfall a year Fewer than 9 people per square kilometre Cattle, sheep, goats and donkeys
■	Dams A Paulo Afonso (1955) B Sobradinho (1979) C Tres Marias (1962)

8 *Water-seller*

9 *Irrigating the cane fields*

FOLLOW-UP WORK

1 Why does the holding of land in latifundia make life hard for most people?
2 Large landowners have physical, financial and political power. Why does this prevent land reform in Brazil?
3 Study the statistics in table (5). Why are large numbers of people leaving the north-east to live in cities in the south-east such as Sao Paulo?
4 Study map (7).
   (a) Why is the interior drier than the coast?
   (b) What changes occur in the number of people and the type of farming as you move inland from the coast?
   (c) Why is there a large river in an area where there is little rainfall?
5 (a) How many different ways could the people use the river before the dams were built?
   (b) How will big dams and reservoirs change these uses of the river?
   (c) Why is irrigation water directed to the latifundia rather than to the minifundia?

Coffee in Brazil

Brazil is the largest producer and exporter of coffee in the world. The drink of coffee is made from the beans of a tropical evergreen bush. Inside each cherry (10) are two peanut-sized beans. It takes the beans of one tree to make one kilogram of coffee. In 1985, Brazil produced 33 million bags of coffee, each bag being 60 kg of green beans. This was one-third of all the coffee grown in the world.

The first coffee seeds and cuttings were brought from French Guiana to the Amazon area of northern Brazil in 1727. At that time, the south was gripped by gold and diamond discoveries and many new towns were growing. By 1800, the gold boom had ended and there were many rich men with money to spend and slaves to put to work. Rio de Janeiro had been made capital city in 1763, in place of Salvador, and coffee growing began in the nearby Paraiba valley (11).

Coffee bushes grow to 9 metres in height and produce fruit for 40 years. As they grow, they take most of the goodness from the soil. When the soils of the Paraiba valley were exhausted, new coffee farms, called fazendas, were made on the interior plateau. Tropical forest and bushland were burnt and coffee bushes were soon growing in neat rows (12). The land was ideal for growing coffee. The deep red soils, called terra roxa, were fertile and well-drained. Gentle slopes helped the soil drain freely. The bushes grew healthily in the hot wet season and the fruit ripened and was harvested in the hot dry season. But after many years of growing coffee, even these fertile soils became exhausted and the coffee-growing area shifted further west and south. Today, most coffee is grown in the areas numbered 3 and 4 on the map.

10 *A branch of ripening coffee cherries*

Coffee growing brought many developments to south-east Brazil. Railways were built to carry coffee beans to the coast. The city of Sao Paulo grew rapidly and Santos became the largest coffee-exporting port in the world.

11 *Migration of coffee growing*

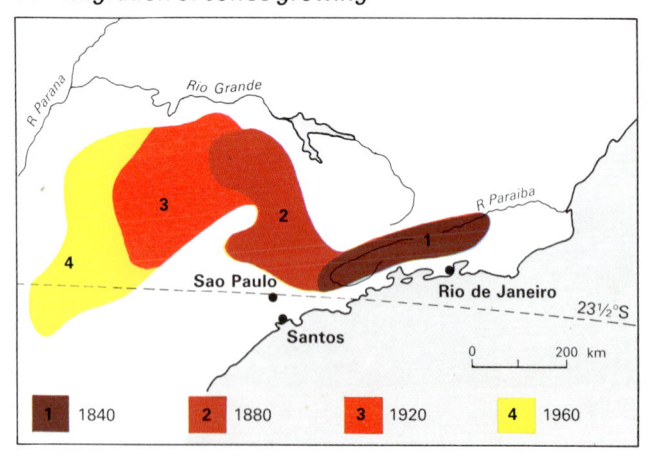

12 *Coffee fazenda*

A coffee fazenda

Coffee fazendas are estates which range in size from 40 to 3000 hectares. The owner or manager lives in a large house at the centre of the estate near to the simple houses of the full-time workers. It is a self-contained community with a school, health clinic, church and meeting room. Each family rents a small plot of land where they grow rice, maize and beans and keep a few pigs and chickens. The family in photograph (13) take care of 5000 coffee bushes. Life is hard and wages low. The children are more likely to be working in the fields than attending school.

In the wet season, the main job is hoeing out the weeds (14). Fertiliser is spread on the soil and the leaves are sprayed to prevent disease. The cherries ripen in the dry season and are ready for picking in July. They can be picked from the branches or collected from the ground. The cherries are thrown in the air (15) to remove any soil, twigs and leaves. A tractor and trailer takes the beans to a central courtyard where they are spread out to dry in the sun.

Bus-loads of hired workers are brought to the fazenda from the favelas on the edge of the city. When the harvest is over, thousands of people are out of work and hungry.

13 A family in the fields

14 Hoeing out the weeds in the wet season

15 Removing leaves and twigs in the dry season

Climatic disasters and coffee prices

On the night of 15 July 1975 when the ripe cherries were almost ready for picking, there was a severe frost. Most of the coffee crop for 1976 was lost and 1000 million trees were killed. This was the worst disaster ever to hit the coffee lands. Growers had to replace dead trees (16) with young seedlings and wait four years for them to bear fruit. More than 1200 million new bushes were planted.

At the time of the disaster, Brazil had 35 million bags of beans in store but these were sold in two years and because there was a shortage of coffee world prices rose. When the new bushes came into production there was more coffee to sell and prices fell.

The worst drought for 40 years hit the coffee-growing region in 1985. As a result, the coffee crop was only 11 million bags in 1986. World coffee prices rose again only to fall in the following years when good harvests returned. These ups and downs in coffee prices are shown in graph (17).

Frost, drought, rain at harvest-time, leaf-disease and the production of too much coffee have been problems for coffee growers in the last 20 years. Many growers have decided to dig up their bushes and grow cotton, sugar cane, soya beans and oranges instead.

16 Coffee bushes hit by frost

CASH CROPS

Cash crops are grown for sale and not for the direct use of the grower. They are often sold to other countries as an export which puts the growers at the mercy of the world market prices.

18 World coffee production (1985–86)

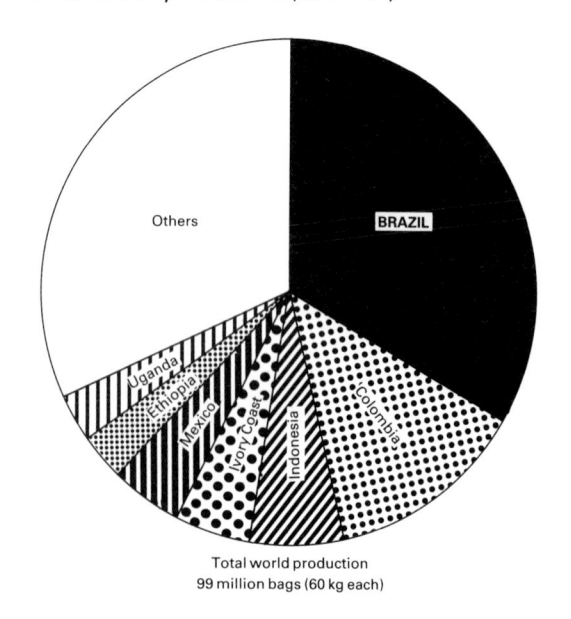

Total world production
99 million bags (60 kg each)

17 Coffee prices

19 Main coffee importers

Country	% of coffee trade
USA	34
West Germany	13
France	9
Italy	6
Japan	5
UK	5
Others	28

Coffee for the world

Brazil is one of more than 40 countries that grow coffee. Seven countries grow two-thirds of world production (18). All these countries grow more coffee than they drink. Brazil consumes one-quarter of production and the rest is shipped to world markets (19, 20).

Coffee is grown in developing countries. Most of these depend on the sale of this one crop to pay for developments in their country (21). Brazil depended on the sale of coffee for more than a hundred years. The export figures for 1985 (22) show the country has developed a wide range of products for export in recent years.

21 Countries relying on coffee exports

Country	% of export earnings made by coffee (1985)
Burundi	97
Uganda	94
El Salvador	73
Rwanda	66
Benin	56
Colombia	51
Ethiopia	50
Central African Republic	46
Guatemala	42
Nicaragua	41
Tanzania	38
Madagascar	38
Costa Rica	33

22 Brazil's exports (by value)

Product	% of total exports
Coffee	10
Soya bean products	10
Iron and steel	9
Transport equipment	7
Iron ore	6
Other ores	6
Beef	6
Machinery	6
Cotton yarn and cloth	4
Chemicals	4
Footwear	4
Electrical equipment	3
Cocoa	2
Office equipment	2
Orange juice	2
Pulp and paper	2
Sugar	2
Tobacco	2
Others	13

20 Coffee at the port of Santos

FOLLOW-UP WORK

1 Copy map (11). Add arrows to show the migration of coffee growing.
2 Why did the trees in the south of the coffee-growing lands suffer the worst frosts?
3 Why are coffee bushes planted in neat rows across the slope of the land (12)?
4 Make a list of the main wet-season jobs and the main dry-season jobs. Study your lists and explain why it is vital to have:
   (a) a wet season and a dry season for coffee growing;
   (b) a large number of workers.
5 Why are prices high when production is low?
6 Why does a frost disaster in Brazil help all the other coffee-growing countries in the world?
7 What dangers are there for a country which depends upon the export of coffee for its development?
8 (a) List Brazil's exports (22) under these headings: agricultural, raw materials, manufactured.
   (b) How do your lists help to show that Brazil is one of the world's most rapidly developing countries?
9 Explain in detail what the person meant who said: 'Coffee is not essential to countries that buy it but is very essential to many countries that sell it'.
10 Coffee is the second most important item, by value, to oil in world trade. Locate the largest producers and consumers of coffee. Ask for the map and exercises.

Sao Paulo: fast-growing city

In 1872, Sao Paulo was a small town of 31 000 people. In 1985, with more than 10 million people, it was the largest city in South America and one of the largest in the world (23). Sao Paulo began to prosper as coffee growing spread across the plateau. Railways were built in all directions to bring coffee through Sao Paulo and its port of Santos to markets of the world. Immigrants from Italy, Portugal, Germany, Spain and Japan came to find work and a new life. They were joined by peasant farmers from the north-east of Brazil. By 1920, Sao Paulo had grown to half a million people and there were grand public buildings, elegant housing areas and many parks and gardens. In 1929, the coffee market in the USA collapsed and the world economic depression began. Wealthy businessmen in Sao Paulo, who had made their fortunes from coffee, invested their money in factories and buildings. Cotton, cattle and food crops on the plateau were the raw materials for cotton cloth, leather goods and food products in the city. From these beginnings, Sao Paulo became the main industrial and business city in Brazil.

The city has grown rapidly since 1950 (23) because new offices and industries have been set up.

24 Skyscrapers in Sao Paulo

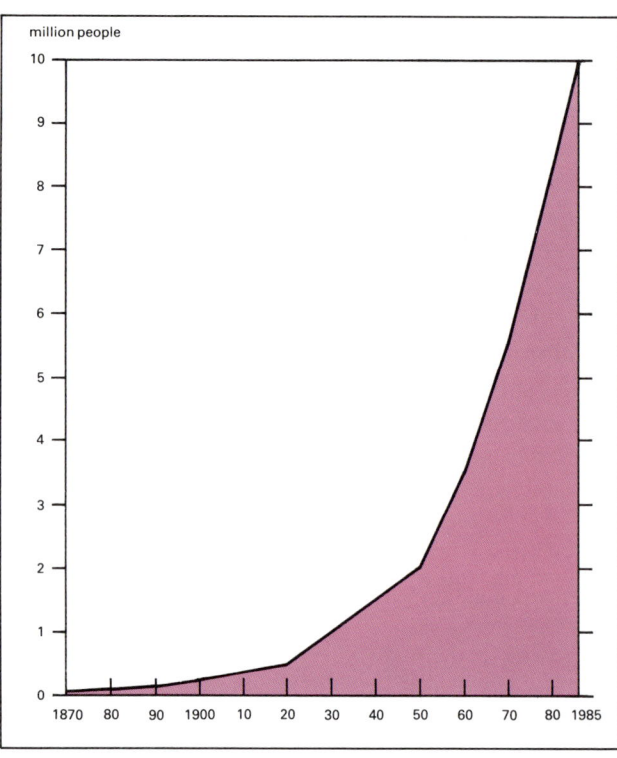

23 Growth of Sao Paulo

National and international companies have their offices in the centre of the city (24). Here you will find the headquarters of 50 banks. There are half a million businesses in the city including 100 000 factories. The biggest of these are international car factories which make a million cars a year. More than 350 000 people each year have crowded into Sao Paulo looking for jobs. Many of them are farmers who have been pushed off their land by large landowners growing sugar cane for car fuel and soya beans for cattle feed on the Sao Paulo plateau. Two million or more have come from the north-east of Brazil, driven from their land by big landowners and by drought.

Sao Paulo is a good location for industry. Hydro-electric power comes from nearby rivers. Capital comes from wealthy businessmen. The large population provides a labour supply and market. Roads and railways radiate from the city, bringing in raw materials and parts and distributing finished products. One of these routes is to the busy port of Santos. There are linked industries where one factory, such as in the car industry, provides the materials or parts for others. You can make a model which shows many of these advantages. Ask for the model sheet.

The fast growth of Sao Paulo has brought with it many problems. Two million people live in favelas (shanty towns) on the outskirts of the city. It is a big task to bring piped water, sewers (25), drains,

> ### URBANISATION
>
> The growth of towns and cities such as Sao Paulo. This is caused by migration from rural areas (countryside) and by the large natural increase of a youthful city population.
> Urbanisation has happened very quickly in Brazil, as the statistics show:
>
> | Year | Population of Brazil Millions | % rural | % urban |
> |---|---|---|---|
> | 1940 | 41 | 69 | 31 |
> | 1950 | 52 | 64 | 36 |
> | 1960 | 71 | 54 | 46 |
> | 1970 | 95 | 44 | 56 |
> | 1980 | 123 | 36 | 64 |
> | 1987 | 142 | 29 | 71 |

electricity, paved roads, street lighting, schools and hospitals to these areas. Only a third of all the homes have drains and only half have piped water. Disease spreads quickly when sewage from cesspools seeps into wells and families drink the water. The city has spread uncontrolled across fertile countryside. Factories are often close to houses, and the noise, smoke and smell damage people's health.

Many thousands of people spend three or four hours a day travelling to and from work between the sprawling suburbs and the city centre, using overcrowded buses on congested roads.

The number of jobs has not kept pace with the number of people coming to the city and the streets are crowded with hawkers, shoe-shiners and beggars.

FOLLOW-UP WORK

1. *A model*
   (a) Bend the wing-shaped sides of the model downwards at right angles along the dashed lines.
   (b) Bend the centre section along the dashed lines to make angles which correspond to the side sections.
   (c) Secure the cross-shaded flaps inside the model with glue or tape.
2. Mark a road onto your model from Sao Paulo to Santos.
   (a) Why is this a very important road?
   (b) What is the main problem for road building?
3. Study the model and say why:
   (a) the climate of Sao Paulo is healthier than the coastal plain area;
   (b) Sao Paulo has a better site and location than Santos for a fast-growing city.

25 *Laying water pipes for a sewage system*

4. The growth of industry in Sao Paulo has been helped by supplies of hydro-electric power.
   (a) Dams were built on the headwaters of the Rio Tiete to make reservoirs near Sao Paulo. Pipelines were laid down the Great Escarpment to a power station near Santos. Mark onto your model a suitable location for this dam, reservoir, pipeline and power station. Write about the advantages for making electricity near Sao Paulo.
   (b) Mark onto your model the sites for three more power stations on any rivers west of Sao Paulo. Give reasons why you chose these sites.
5. Traffic congestion is a problem in Sao Paulo. The streets are packed with cars and buses.
   (a) Explain how big office blocks at the centre of the city:
      (i) help to cause traffic congestion at certain times of the day;
      (ii) stop the building of better roads.
   (b) Decide ways of easing the problems of traffic congestion in the centre of the city.
6. Show by labelled drawings
   (a) the advantages for industry in Sao Paulo,
   (b) the problems of living there.

TOPIC FOR DISCUSSION: FOOD OR FUEL

In 1975, when Brazil imported 80 per cent of all the oil used, the government began a scheme to make alcohol from sugar cane. The alcohol is mixed with petrol for cars and lorries.

Sugar cane is now grown on 10 per cent of Brazil's cropland, replacing food crops grown by small farmers, who have moved into Sao Paulo.

Although the cost of making alcohol is high, the scheme has provided thousands of jobs in 300 distilleries. Oil has now been found in the Amazon forest and off the coast of Rio de Janeiro. Should the alcohol scheme continue?

Industry in Brazil

Brazil's idea of development has been one of rapid industrial growth. There has been much less concern for the well-being of large numbers of Brazilians who live in poverty.

In a little over 50 years the country has moved through the four stages of industrial development shown in figure (26). By the mid 1980s Brazil had become the world's seventh largest steel producer, ninth largest producer of cars and third largest shipbuilder. Manufactures, which represented only 10 per cent of exports in 1971, had risen to 50 per cent in 1986.

Iron and steel

Steel is needed for buildings and bridges, to make cars and ships, for pipelines, railways, cables and machinery. The growth of the steel industry and the uses for steel are shown in tables (27) and (28).

The country's main advantage for making steel is her vast supply of iron ore. Much of this is found in south-east Brazil in the state of Minas Gerais. It is high-grade ore with 68 per cent iron content. It is easily mined from open pits (29).

Brazil is short of coal. Poor quality coal is mined in the south of Brazil. This coal has to be mixed with good coking coal imported from the USA before it can be used in the blast furnace.

Brazil's steelworks are located in the south-east near to the iron ore mines and the three largest cities, Sao Paulo, Rio de Janeiro and Belo Horizonte. Study the map of this area (30) and attempt the questions that follow.

26 *Four stages of industrial development*

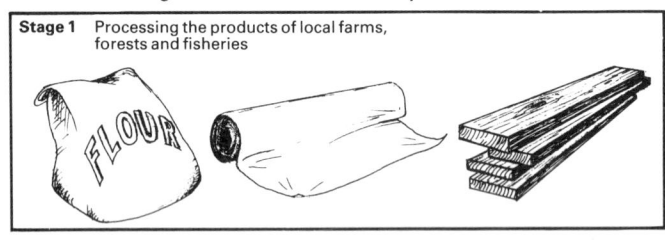

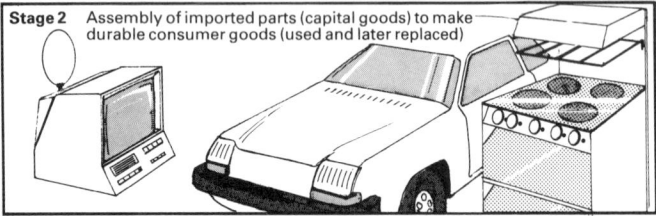

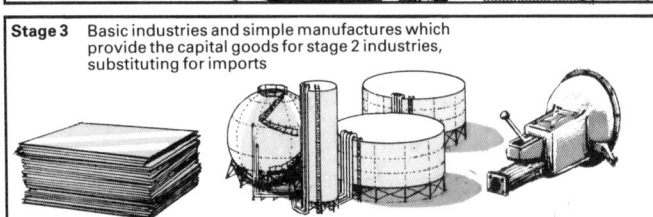

Stage 1 Processing the products of local farms, forests and fisheries

Stage 2 Assembly of imported parts (capital goods) to make durable consumer goods (used and later replaced)

Stage 3 Basic industries and simple manufactures which provide the capital goods for stage 2 industries, substituting for imports

Stage 4 Manufacture of machinery, technology products and factory installations for own use and for export

27 *Steel production*

Year	Million tonnes
1960	2
1965	3
1970	5
1975	8
1980	15
1985	20

28 *Uses for steel in Brazil*

Use	% of steel used
Buildings and bridges	25
Vehicles	20
Machinery	11
Wire and cables	10
Pipeline and tubes	8
Cans and containers	7
Railways	6
Ships	5
Household appliances	4
Farm machinery and equipment	3
Others	1

29 *Iron ore mine near Belo Horizonte*

31 Furnas HEP station

30 Location of steelworks

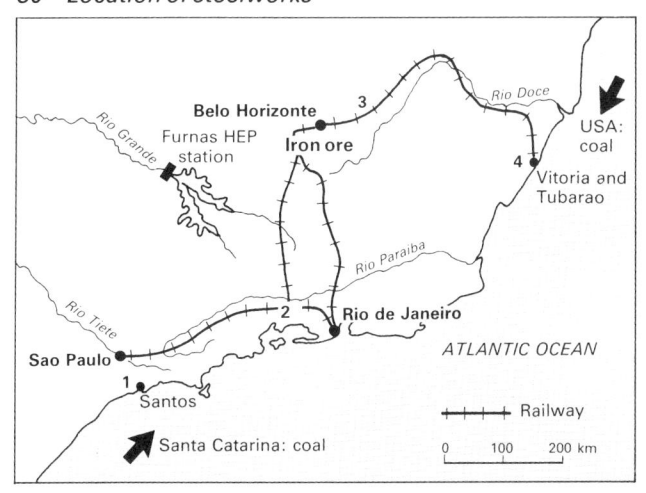

FOLLOW-UP WORK

1. Which ports shown on map (30) have the best location for the export of iron ore to the USA and Europe?
2. Limestone and manganese are both found in the area of the map. Why does this help the steel industry?
3. Why has Furnas HEP station (31) a good location to supply electricity to the steel industry?
4. (a) Copy chart (32). Complete the chart with details of the main factors affecting the location of each steelworks. Site 1 has been done for you.
   (b) Which of the four towns has the best location for a steelworks? Give reasons for your answer.

32 Factors affecting the location of steelworks

Site	Town	Coal	Iron ore	Market
1	Piacaguera near Santos	Nearest to the Santa Catarina coalfields	Far away – 500 km by rail	Near to Sao Paulo, the largest market for steel
2	Volta Redonda			
3	Ipatinga			
4	Tubarao			

Multinational companies in Brazil

Industrial development has been achieved with the help of multinational companies (33, 34) which have their headquarters in the USA, UK, West Germany, Italy, Japan and other developed countries in the North. These companies set up factories in Brazil because of the promise of good profits, low taxes, low costs of land, labour, electricity, steel and materials and a large home market.

Ford, General Motors and Volkswagen built car factories in towns near Sao Paulo and Fiat built at Belo Horizonte. Their factories not only produce cars for the big home market but also for other countries in South America and the developing world. The cost of making cars and lorries is low and large numbers are exported to Europe. Ishikawajima of Japan and Verolme of the Netherlands built shipyards in Brazil at Rio de Janeiro and Angra dos Reis (35, 36). Ninety per cent of the ships that are built are bought by the government or by private companies in Brazil. Oil tankers, bulk-carriers, cargo liners and container ships help to carry Brazil's growing trade. The new car and shipbuilding industries are capital-intensive (37). Some people think this is not the appropriate type of industry for developing countries. Study chart (38) which shows some of the advantages and problems of multinationals.

35 *Ishibras shipyard, Rio de Janeiro*

> **MULTINATIONAL COMPANY**
>
> A company which has branch factories and operations in other countries.
>
> In Brazil there are few industries where foreign countries control less than half of the production, employment and profits.

33 Some multinational companies in Brazil

Company	Country	Employment	Product
Volkswagen	W. Germany	35 500	Cars
Ford	USA	21 300	Cars
General Motors	USA	19 000	Cars
Fiat	Italy	13 000	Cars
Firestone	USA	13 000	Rubber and plastics
Pirelli	Italy	12 700	
Mannesmann	W. Germany	11 000	Machines
Philco	USA	9 500	Radio/TV
Verolme	Netherlands	7 000	Ships
Johnson & Johnson	USA	6 400	Pharmaceuticals
Unilever	UK/Netherlands	5 800	Detergent
Alcan	Canada	5 500	Aluminium

34 Control by multinational companies

Industry	Employment by multinational companies (% of total)
Cars	100
Car components	50
Tractors	70
Household goods	65
Electrical goods	85
Office equipment	65
Chemicals	60
Plastics	50
Rubber	70
Industrial machinery	55

36 Location of shipyards

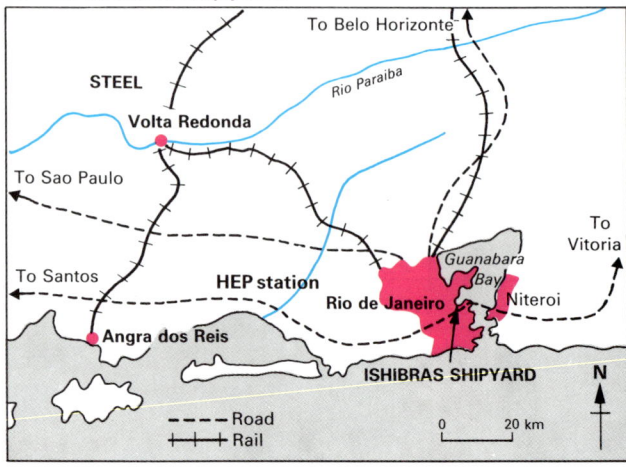

ADVANTAGES

1. Brazil gains modern industries direct from the developed world.
   This widens the base of the economy.
2. The country no longer needs to import all its manufactured goods from other countries.
3. There are thousands of jobs in the factories and, by linkage, in other plants which supply materials and parts, for example.
4. Wages are often higher than for other jobs bringing better living standards for many people.
5. The company spends money on buildings, houses, clinics and schools, for example.

PROBLEMS

1. The government has little control over the company. Decisions are made in the home country. If profits are small, the factory can be taken away as quickly as it was set up.
2. The company aims to make high profits from international operations. Most earnings are taken out of the country.
3. Jobs may be lost in local traditional industries, such as textiles, if there is competition with the new factory.
4. The company benefits from low labour costs and may pull out if this changes.
5. Brazil borrowed heavily from other countries to set up industries. Rising world interest rates has resulted in big debts.

38 Multinationals: advantages and problems

FOLLOW-UP WORK

1. Suggest reasons why multinational companies have built factories in Brazil and not in many other countries in South America.
   Consider these: location/size of country/size of population/hard-working people with a national identity/wealth from farming/mineral and power resources/infrastructure such as roads/government help.
2. Study the advantages and problems of multinationals shown in figure (38). Choose two of each of these which you consider the most important. Give your reasons.
3. What advantages are there for locating
   (a) car factories in the Sao Paulo area;
   (b) shipyards at Rio de Janeiro (36)?
4. Explain how the shipyard, built by Japan (35), benefits (a) Brazil, (b) Japan.

37 Cutting steel plate at the shipyard

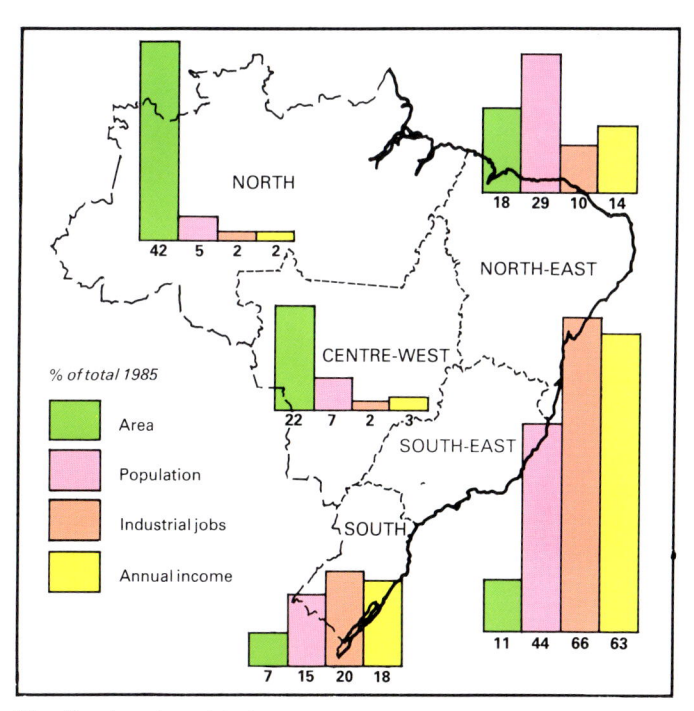

39 Regional contrasts

5. Study map (39). Which region of Brazil
   (a) is the poorest;
   (b) is the richest;
   (c) has the most industry?
6. What might be the advantages and problems of concentrating industry in one region (part) of the country?

STRUCTURE OF EMPLOYMENT

The share of workers in primary, secondary and tertiary jobs. This has changed in Brazil in the last 50 years as industrial development has taken place. (Ask for the activity sheet.)

Developing the interior: Brasilia

In the sixteenth century the Portuguese settled along the coast of Brazil. In the sugar boom of the seventeenth century the north-east coast became the most settled area. In the eighteenth century, mining brought people to the south-east coast. Coffee was the most important product in the nineteenth century, which led to the rapid growth of Rio de Janeiro and Sao Paulo. Industrial development this century has provided jobs and social benefits in the same area. The three cities of Sao Paulo, Rio de Janeiro and Belo Horizonte form a 'golden triangle' of industry, business and wealth (40). Large areas of the interior are remote, inhospitable and undeveloped.

These geographical and historical factors help to explain why most people still live on or near to the coast and why the interior is sparsely settled. This is shown on the population density map (41).

Since the 1950s new roads have been built to spread development beyond the golden triangle across dry scrubland (42) and into the Amazon forest which covers almost half of Brazil. People pushed off their land by landowners growing soya and sugar cane have followed the roadbuilders into the interior.

Certain points in the interior were chosen for big development projects. These are growth poles. Brasilia is one of them.

In 1956, the government decided that a new capital city, called Brasilia, would be built near the middle of Brazil to replace Rio de Janeiro. New government offices would be built, new roads would radiate in all directions and new developments would begin.

An area of gently rolling land was chosen as the site for the new city. It was an empty land with poor soils and scrub vegetation. There were rivers near the site for a water supply and limestone rock to make concrete buildings. Supplies were brought in by air before roads reached the site 1000 kilometres from Rio de Janeiro.

Brasilia became capital city in 1960. In 1986, 1 600 000 people lived there and in nearby towns. There is a big contrast between life in the well-planned city and that in the favelas of the satellite towns. Many people have mixed feelings about the quality of life in the new city with its wide roads, blocks of flats and wide open spaces. The city has achieved its main aim to bring development to the interior.

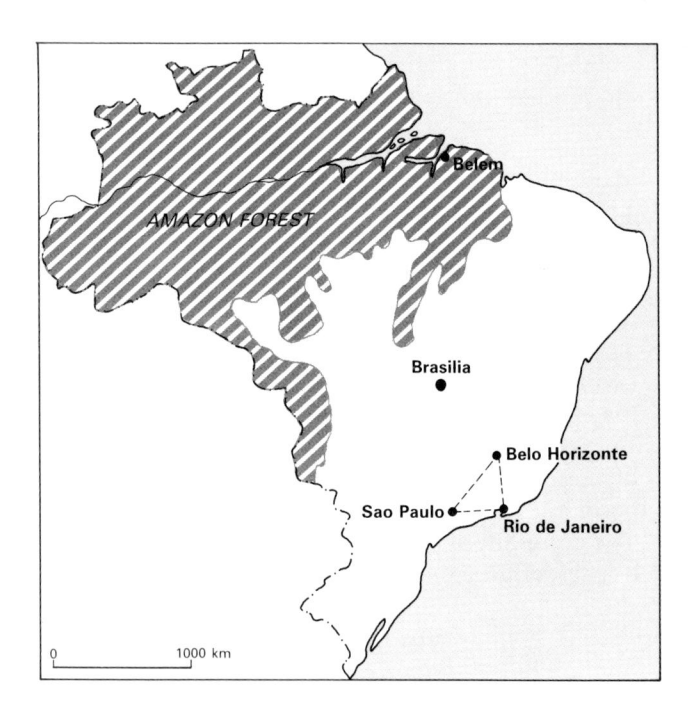

40 Brasilia and the Amazon forest

41 Population density and ten largest cities

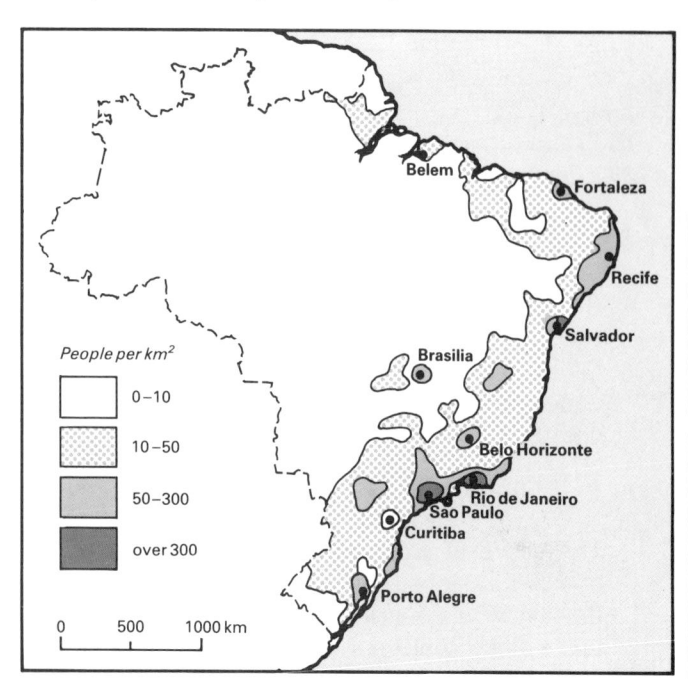

GROWTH POLE

A place where economic growth is started and stimulated by building roads, providing electricity, opening factories and developing resources.

POPULATION DENSITY

The average number of people living in an area, such as 1 square kilometre. The highest densities are in Brazil's ten largest cities shown on map (41).

Where are the lowest densities? Explain why.

42 Road across the dry interior ▶

FOLLOW-UP WORK

1 Re-arrange the middle and end parts of the following sentences to make five correct statements about the plan of Brasilia.

	District		Location		Reason
1	The area of hospitals and community centres	A	lies to the west of the city centre	a	because it is a prominent place for the city's main function.
2	The industrial district	B	is in the southern part of the city	b	close to the main housing area it serves.
3	The business district	C	is along the north-south axis	c	near to the railway and far away from the houses.
4	The area of government buildings	D	is near the centre of Brasilia	d	where there is plenty of space near the lake and centre of government.
5	The area of foreign embassies	E	is in the east-west axis	e	because it needs to be accessible from all parts of the city.

43 The business district

2 Imagine that you have the job of completing the plan of Brasilia. Sites 1 to 7 on plan (45) are available for the following developments: the president's palace, zoo, warehouses, bus station, airport, secondary school, university. Choose a site for each development and give the reasons for your decisions.

3 Study plan (45).
 (a) Give one advantage and one disadvantage
   (i) for locating the industrial district a long distance from the housing areas;
   (ii) for building wide roads set in large open spaces;
   (iii) for living by the side of the lake.
 (b) Suggest three different uses for the lake and its dam.

4 Study photographs (43), (44) and (46).
 (a) Over which point on the map was the aeroplane positioned when the photograph (46) was taken?
 (b) Why are the office blocks built higher than the blocks of flats?
 (c) Why are the blocks of flats on stilts?

5 Suggest one reason for each of the following:
 (a) Many people who live in Brasilia were forced to live there.
 (b) Many people who have chosen to move to Brasilia live in towns outside the city.
 (c) Brasilia has a good location as a capital city of a developing country.

44 Blocks of flats

37

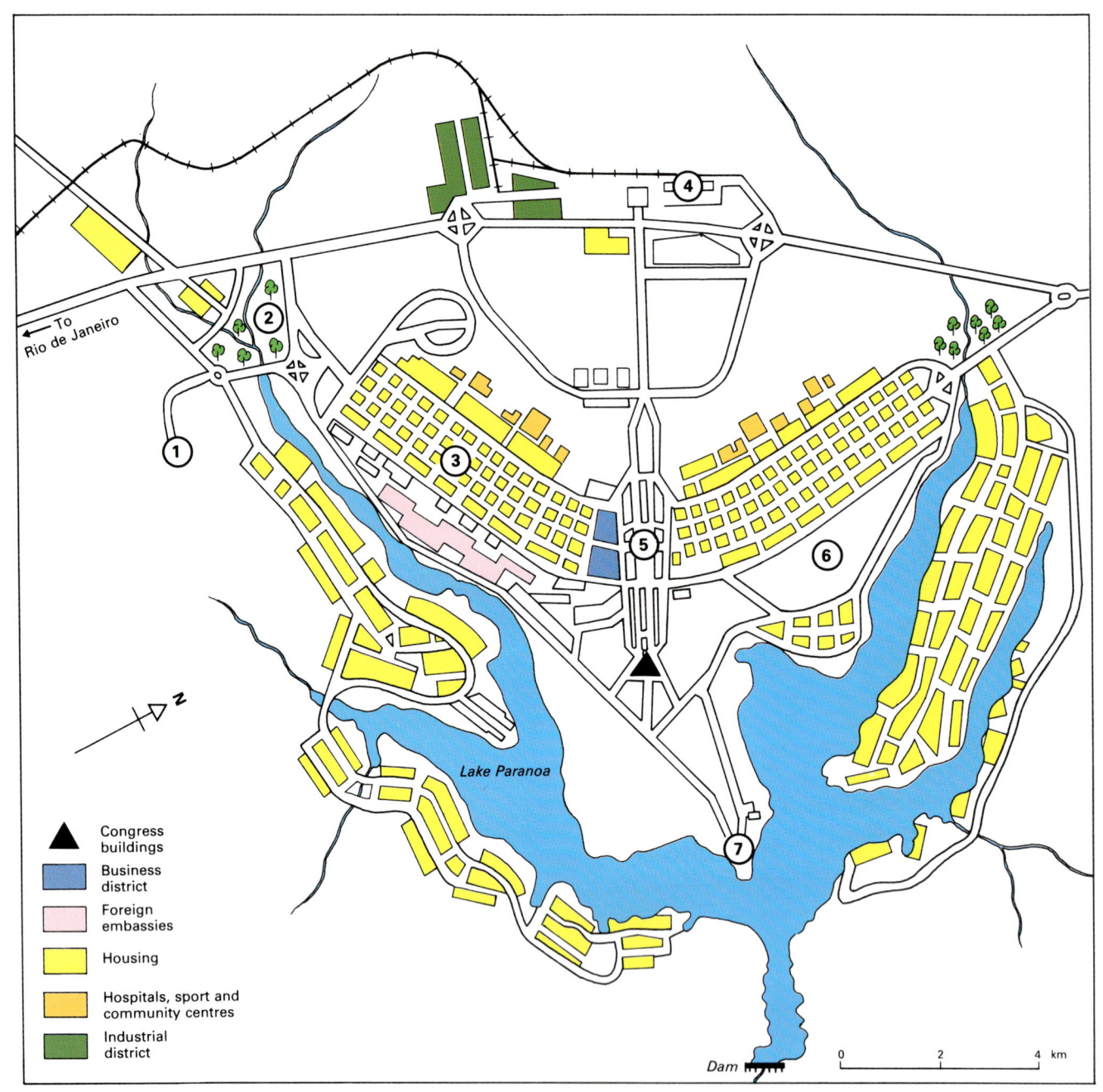

45 Plan of Brasilia

The plan of Brasilia is based on two axes which make the shape of a cross. One axis is curved to follow the contour of the land and the shape of the lake which was formed by damming the river. The city is divided into separate areas of housing, government, business and industry. There are wide roads and large open spaces with lawns, gardens, fountains and modern sculptures.

46 One axis of the city

Opening up the forest

At the same time Brasilia was being built, a road was cut through the Amazon forest from Brasilia to Belem. This is the spine road of Brazil, linking the undeveloped north to the developed south. The road was completed in 1960. Within ten years the number of people living between Brasilia and Belem increased from 100 000 to 2 million. One hundred new settlements grew up along the road. At first they were truck and restaurant stops and camp sites for road workers, but soon they had grown into towns with shops, churches and schools. Peasants from the north-east began to grow rice, beans, maize and cotton on small plots of land. Most land was bought by cattle ranchers who cut and burnt the trees and soon had 5 million head of cattle grazing freshly-sown pastures. The opening up of the Amazon forest had begun.

Near to the Equator the sun is never far from overhead and temperatures are a constant 27 °C to 30 °C. The heat causes the moisture-laden air to rise and there are torrential downpours of rain. This is convectional rainfall. It is very wet when the sun is overhead. The northern tributaries of the Amazon river are in flood in June and the southern tributaries flood in December. Evergreen trees never stop growing in these hot and wet conditions. Most of them grow 20 to 40 metres high and the giant tree in photograph (47) is 50 metres high. The trees are close together and their branches and leaves are at the top forming a canopy which blots out the light from the ground where few plants grow. Lianas are flowering shrubs in clearings, but in the forest they grow rapidly upwards to get the sunlight (48), often lacing the trees together. Rivers were the only way into the forest (49) until the bulldozers cut their way through to Belem.

47 Inside the forest

48 Lianas reach for the light

49 The Amazon river downstream from Manaus

Roads and farms in the forest

The Trans-Amazonian Highway was cut through the rainforest between 1970 and 1973 (50). It stretches more than 5000 kilometres from the north-east coast of Brazil to the border of Peru (51). The highway links towns on the tributaries south of the Amazon to make a network of river and road transport.

It was planned to settle 100 000 families along the highway. This would be the start of a new life for people of the north-east forced off their tiny plots of land by a drought in 1970. Each family was given a 100-hectare plot of land and a two-roomed wooden house for a total cost of £400 to be re-paid over 20 years. The houses were built either along the highway or on side roads in a small community (agrovila) of fifty families. Each agrovila was to have a primary school, health clinic, and store. Each farmer was given six months' wages to grow his crop of manioc, maize, rice and beans and raise a few pigs and chickens.

50 *The Trans-Amazonian Highway*

In 1974, only 5000 families had been settled when the government abandoned the scheme. Life has been hard for the new settlers. The plots of land had not been cleared of trees. Many plots were a 10-kilometre walk from the agrovila. The health clinics were often not built and children died from malaria and dysentery. The biggest problem was the land itself.

51 *Highways across the forest*

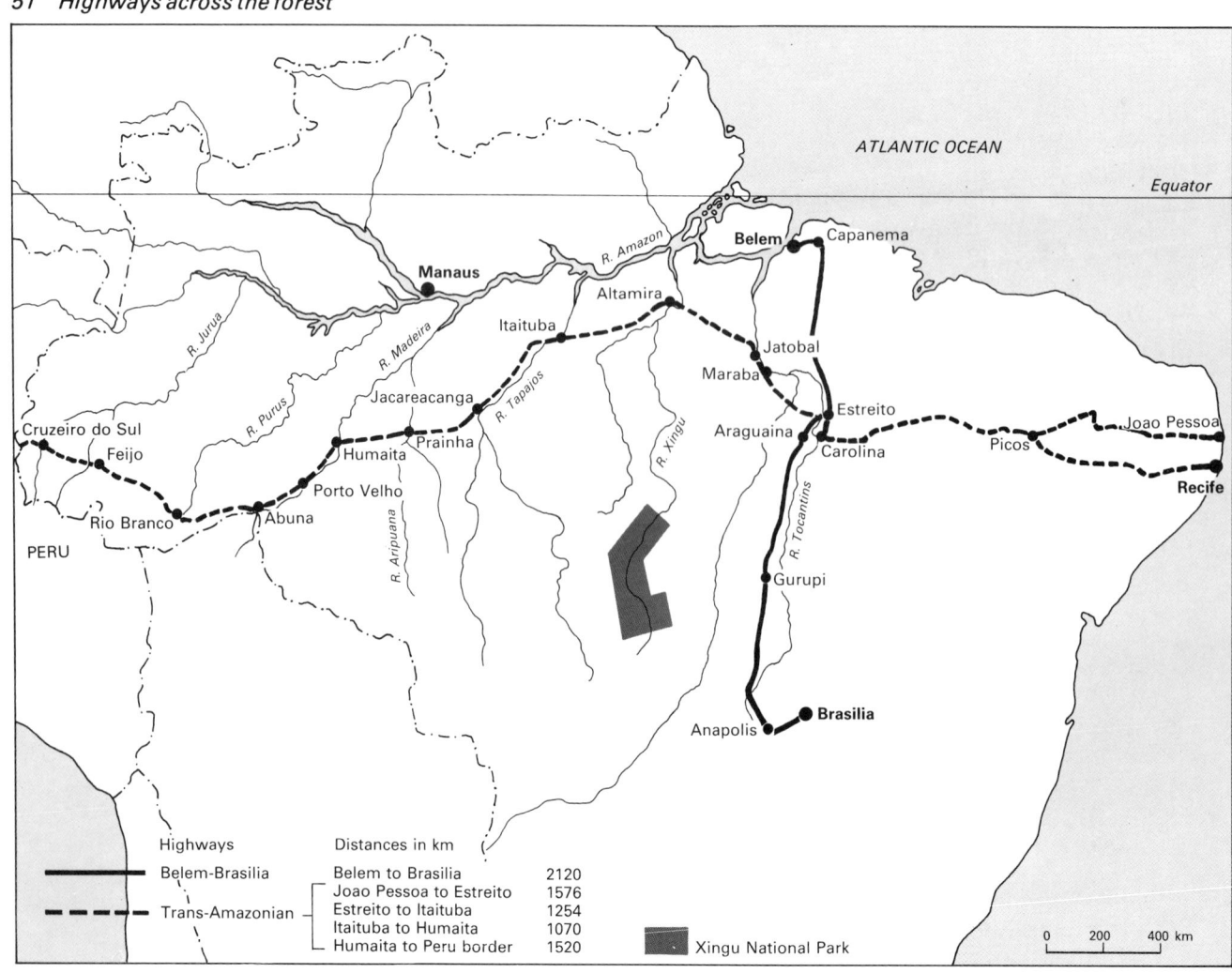

Distances in km	
Belem to Brasilia	2120
Joao Pessoa to Estreito	1576
Estreito to Itaituba	1254
Itaituba to Humaita	1070
Humaita to Peru border	1520

ECOSYSTEM

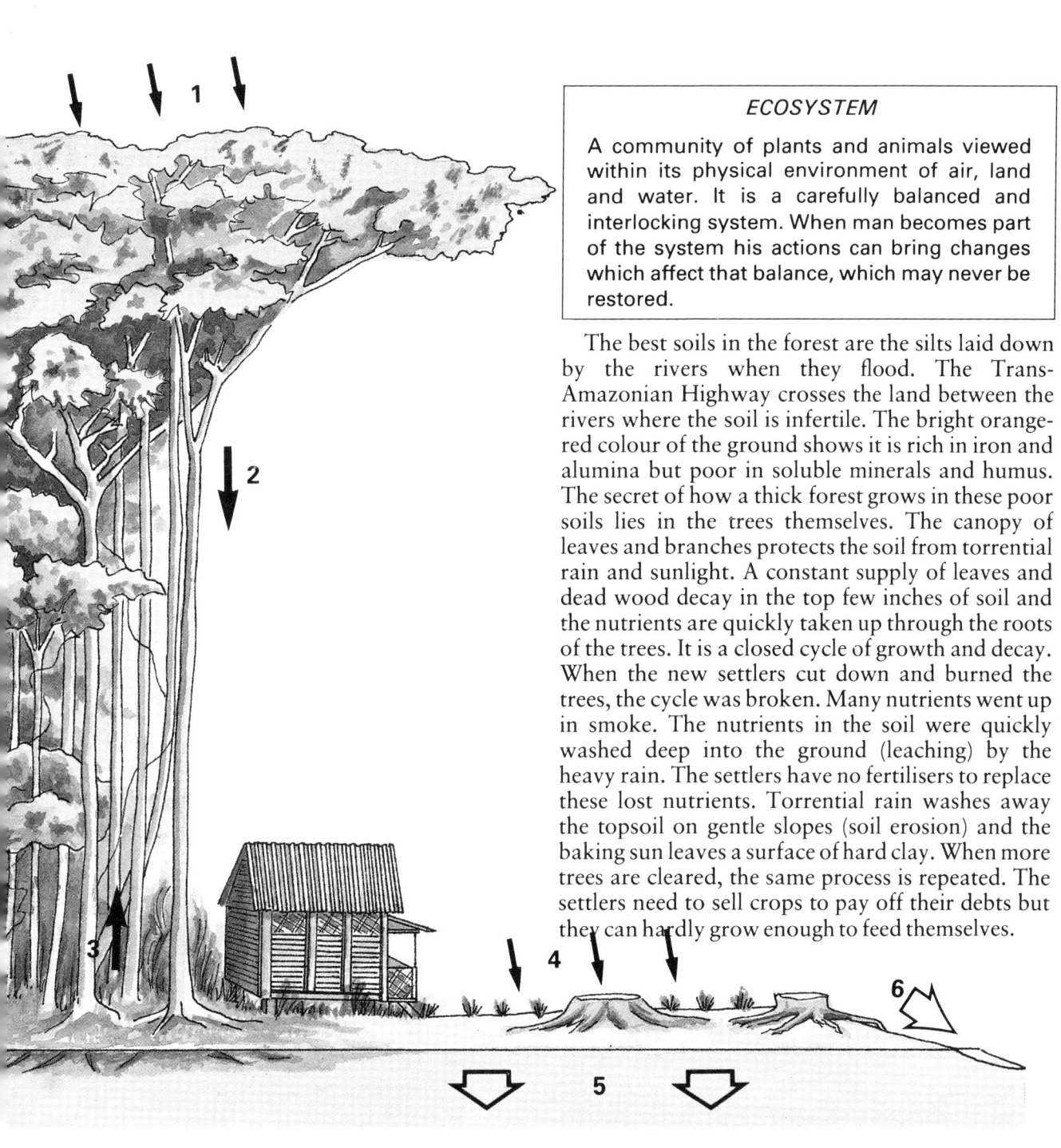

A community of plants and animals viewed within its physical environment of air, land and water. It is a carefully balanced and interlocking system. When man becomes part of the system his actions can bring changes which affect that balance, which may never be restored.

The best soils in the forest are the silts laid down by the rivers when they flood. The Trans-Amazonian Highway crosses the land between the rivers where the soil is infertile. The bright orange-red colour of the ground shows it is rich in iron and alumina but poor in soluble minerals and humus. The secret of how a thick forest grows in these poor soils lies in the trees themselves. The canopy of leaves and branches protects the soil from torrential rain and sunlight. A constant supply of leaves and dead wood decay in the top few inches of soil and the nutrients are quickly taken up through the roots of the trees. It is a closed cycle of growth and decay. When the new settlers cut down and burned the trees, the cycle was broken. Many nutrients went up in smoke. The nutrients in the soil were quickly washed deep into the ground (leaching) by the heavy rain. The settlers have no fertilisers to replace these lost nutrients. Torrential rain washes away the topsoil on gentle slopes (soil erosion) and the baking sun leaves a surface of hard clay. When more trees are cleared, the same process is repeated. The settlers need to sell crops to pay off their debts but they can hardly grow enough to feed themselves.

52 Farm in the forest

FOLLOW-UP WORK

1 Study map (51).
  (a) What is the total length of the Trans-Amazonian Highway?
  (b) A truck is carrying supplies from Joao Pessoa to a new tin mining area at Humaita.
    (i) What is the length of this journey in kilometres?
    (ii) If the truck travels 250 kilometres each day, how many days will the journey take?
    (iii) What problems will the driver face on unsurfaced sections of road if he goes in December?

2 The forest covers 4 million square kilometres; the United Kingdom is 250 000 square kilometres. How many times would the United Kingdom fit into the forest?

3 Do a simple sketch of the farm in the forest (52). Add the following notes in the correct places (1 to 6).
  Soil erosion on gentle slopes
  Sun and rain on the canopy
  Nutrients taken up by the trees
  Falling leaves return nutrients to the soil
  Sun and rain on the land
  Nutrients are leached downwards

Projects in the forest

The Jari project

In 1967, bulldozers began knocking down trees along the Jari river. Huge fires were started and the seedlings of the melina tree were planted in the ashes of the natural forest. This was the beginning of the Jari project located 400 kilometres west of Belem (53). The aim of the project is to make pulp to supply the paper industry in Europe and the USA. It was begun by an American businessman who bought 16 000 square kilometres of land from the Brazilian government. He found the melina tree growing at the rapid rate of four metres a year in Nigeria and brought the species to Brazil. The tree did well on clay soil but died on the sandy soils which had to be planted with Caribbean pines. Four thousand labourers were brought to the site from the north-east of Brazil. They had to learn how to handle a chain saw, clean out the weeds and build roads and houses.

In ten years, the first tree plantations were ready to cut and make into pulp. One of the largest pulpmills in the world was made in a shipyard in Japan. It was mounted onto two floating platforms and towed 25 000 kilometres across the Indian and Atlantic oceans to a landing site on the Jari river (54). The factory took sixteen months to make and three months to tow to Brazil. In 1979, the mill began the production of 750 tonnes of sheet pulp per day (55), using 2000 tonnes of wood.

The Jari project includes rice farming on 14 000 hectares of the Amazon floodplain. Rice seeds, herbicides, pesticides and fertilisers are all spread by a light aircraft. Rice harvesting is done by a fleet of combine harvesters brought from the USA. One of the world's most hostile areas has been made productive.

The project is faced with many problems. Trees cannot be grown fast enough to meet the needs of the pulpmill. Tree growth is slowing down as the nutrients disappear from the soil. The melina tree has been struck by disease and tropical eucalyptus trees are being planted in their place. Life is very hard for the forest workers. They live in a shanty town on the banks of the river or sling their hammocks in a forest camp. On the opposite bank, the business staff and technicians, who come from the USA, Canada, Japan and southern cities of Brazil, live in the new town of Monte Dourado. Here there are luxury prefabricated houses, medical centres, schools and a supermarket. In 1982, the project had still to make a profit when the American businessman sold back to the Brazilian government this huge area of the Amazon rainforest.

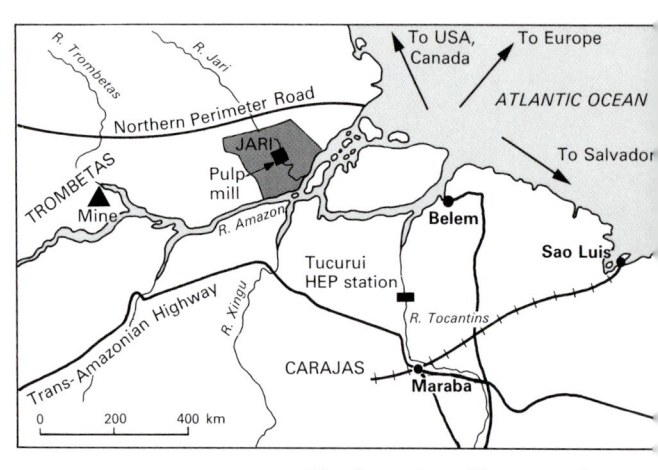

53 Location of forest projects

54 Towing the power plant up Jari river

Mining projects

The new roads which have been cut through the rainforest have led to the discovery of aluminium, iron, copper, tin, nickel, gold, silver and oil. The mining of bauxite (aluminium ore) began near the Trombetas river in 1979 (53). The rock is very easily mined at the surface (56). The ore is carried 30 kilometres by rail to Porto Trombetas. From there bulk carrier ships take much of the ore to large smelters at Belem and Sao Luis. Alcan Aluminium company of Canada partly owns the mines and half of the ore goes to its smelter at Jonquiére in Quebec.

The world's largest known reserves of iron ore are in the hills of Carajas between the Xingu and Tocantins rivers (53). The high grade (66 per cent) iron ore can be scooped out from the surface, without blasting, down to a depth of 400 metres and within a radius of 70 kilometres. An 890-kilometre electric railway has been built to the Atlantic port of Sao Luis. The first shipment was in 1986. It is planned to carry 30 million tonnes of ore each year along the track. Most of this will be exported, mainly to Japan, West Germany and Italy. Power for the mines, railway and smelters comes from the Tucurui HEP station on the Tocantins river. This was the first major power station in the Amazon region when it began producing electricity in 1985. More power stations are planned for the Tocantins and Xingu rivers.

Carajas is a 'superproject' which already includes iron ore and manganese mining. There are also plans for mining copper, nickel, gold and silver and for growing crops and raising cattle. The whole scheme covers an area of 150 000 square kilometres. A great deal of forest will disappear as the project expands.

55 Pulpmill in operation on the site

DEFORESTATION

The removal of a forest.

Large areas of the Amazon rainforest are being lost to farming, mining, roads and reservoirs as well as cutting for timber and fuel.

The world is losing tropical rainforest at a rapid rate. (Ask for details.)

---

56 Mining bauxite at Trombetas

Cattle rearing projects

Large areas of the Amazon rainforest, particularly in the south and east, have been cleared for cattle ranches (57). New roads, cheap land, cheap labour and the high price for beef has meant big profits for big companies burning down the forest. It is estimated that an area the size of England (130 000 km^2) has been cleared of forest since the 1960s, to support up to 10 million cattle. The cleared land is used for from five to eight years before the soil has lost its fertility and is abandoned.

Most of the meat is exported to the USA for beefburgers and to Britain for corned beef, for example.

Many people are worried that cattle rearing is replacing forest. Some of their reasons are shown in figure (58).

57 Cattle ranching replaces the rainforest

A   LOSS OF SOIL FERTILITY: Rainwater leaches away the nutrients from the upper layer of the soil. The trees are no longer there to retain the nutrients.
B   SOIL EROSION: Heavy rain washes away the soil which no longer has the protection of the forest canopy and tree roots.
C   FLOODS: Trees no longer soak up water to be returned to the atmosphere through the leaves (transpiration). Rivers heavily laden with silt quickly overflow their banks.
D   PERMANENT FOREST LOSS: Trees may never return to abandoned ranches because of the damage to the soil and the scale of clearing.
E   LOSS OF PLANT SPECIES: Plant species may be lost which might have provided medicines and drugs to fight disease.
F   LOSS OF WILDLIFE: Wildlife dies out as habitats are destroyed. Some animal species could become extinct.
G   LOSS OF INDIAN TRIBES: Forest tribes die out as their forest environment is destroyed.
H   CLIMATIC CHANGES: Burning forests releases carbon. Carbon dioxide traps heat in the atmosphere (the 'greenhouse effect'). This may be changing rainfall patterns in the world, bringing unusual droughts or floods.

58 The problems of deforestation

FOLLOW-UP WORK

1 Rank the list of problems caused by deforestation. Give your reasons for the order of importance you choose.
2 'The advantages of clearing the forest for development projects such as mining, oil exploration, cattle rearing and providing new homes and farms for poor landless families from north-east Brazil outweigh the problems shown in figure (58).' Do you agree? Give your reasons.
3 'The only reason for using the Jari region of the Amazon was cheap land. This is a very poor reason for destroying rainforest, wildlife and the lives of the original settlers.' Study the details of the Jari project and make lists of:
   (a) the advantages of the area for a tree-farming project;
   (b) the problems for tree farming;
   (c) where the project obtained:
      (i) a fast-growing pulp tree;
      (ii) power station and pulp mill;
      (iii) farm machinery;
      (iv) labourers;
      (v) technicians;
      (vi) markets for the pulp.
Study your lists and then write your opinions about the statement above.
4 In what ways is the Carajas iron ore mining project a better or worse development than the Jari project?
5 A family has been pushed off the land in north-east Brazil. They have decided to seek a new life elsewhere in Brazil. They are thinking about the following places to go: the city of Sao Paulo; to an agrovila in the Amazon; to the Carajas project. Use your knowledge of Brazil to decide where the family should go.

The Amazon Indians

59 Outside a communal house

Indians have been living in the rainforest for 15 000 years. Small tribal groups live in villages scattered through the forest. Waura Indians live in the upper part of the Xingu river valley.

Photograph (59) shows a maloca which is a communal house shared by four families. There are five malocas around the central square cleared of trees and bushes.

Communal effort helps the Indians to survive in the forest. They share the land, their food and work. The men catch fish from the river by beating the water with long poles from their dug-out canoes. This drives the fish into nets and traps. The men also collect wild fruit from the forest and sometimes bring in a deer or monkey to add to their diet. The basic food is the manioc root which the women grow in small clearings in the forest. A small garden is made by cutting and burning the trees. The soil is not turned, the weeds are not removed from the surface and the surrounding trees shade the soil. After two or three years the garden is allowed to overgrow and a new patch is cleared and cultivated. This is called shifting cultivation.

The manioc root is peeled, soaked in water, squeezed in a wooden press to remove poisonous juices, dried and then grilled into cakes on a plate of clay (60). The same roots are used to make soup and beer.

The Indians' way of life is threatened by modern developments. When a new road passes through the tribal lands, government officials contact the tribe, bring medical aid and warn the Indians to keep away from the road. The danger is not the traffic, because there is little, but alcohol and disease brought by the road workers and settlers. When members of the tribal group become ill, the community cannot function properly, food supplies become scarce and the group dies out. Before the arrival of Europeans in the sixteenth century there were 4 million Indians; today there are 120 000. In 1900 there were 260 tribes and today there are 143.

The Indians are in the path of an advancing frontier of cattle farming. Since the 1960s the cattle frontier has spread north and west of Brasilia across the savanna lands and into the rainforest. The government has sold huge blocks of land to big companies to make the land productive. One ranch alone cover 8000 square kilometres. The trees were cut and burnt, 15 000 Zebu cows put to graze on grass sown in the ashes, and 260 Indians were moved into a mission station. Neither the forest with its wildlife nor the Indians who live there are allowed to stand in the way of the cattlemen.

60 Grilling cakes of manioc

TOPIC FOR DISCUSSION: SURVIVAL

The Xingu National Park was created by the government in 1961. It is 13 500 square kilometres of rainforest in the middle of the Xingu valley (see page 40). It was to be a protected area where a dozen tribes of primitive Indians could live in peace and safety.

There would be some contact with outsiders. There would be a medical post and schools, and the Indians could have simple metal objects such as fishing hooks and knives. In this way the Indians would gradually be introduced to the civilisation they would eventually join.

In 1971, the cattle frontier reached the park. A road was planned through the northern part of the park at a good crossing point of the river. This was part of a route from Brasilia to the Trans-Amazonian Highway system. The land to the north of the road would be used to raise cattle. This land would be replaced by extra land added to the south of the park. One village of the Txukahamae tribe would need to be moved but their other village would lie just inside the northern boundary of the park.

A government debate took place to consider the arguments in favour of and against the road. The cattle ranchers claimed that the road must pass through the park because it extended 500 kilometres down the valley, blocking the direct route to market. The road was considered vital to carry the trucks of meat to markets in the south plus exports to the USA and Europe. The National Park Committee argued that the road should be re-routed either to the north or south of the park to avoid disturbing the Indians. They felt that the survival of the Indian race depended on this decision.

Your classroom debate

Four speakers are required: two speak on behalf of the National Highway Department who will argue for the planned road, and two represent the National Park Committee who will argue against the scheme as planned. Each speaker has a few minutes to put his case to the class and each seconder can add extra points, following a class discussion. A vote is taken at the end of the debate to decide whether a road should be built across the Xingu National Park.

Ask for the real outcome of the debate.

61 Indian in the forest

Zambia

A mining country

A railway is the backbone of Zambia (1). It was built between 1905 and 1909 by the British South Africa Company. The railway linked the lead and zinc mine at Broken Hill (now Kabwe) and copper mines further north to ports in South Africa. The line also gave Britain control over the centre of Africa and stopped Germany and Portugal spreading their control across the continent.

Africans were moved away from the land on both sides of the railway to make way for settlers. The settlers grew maize and reared beef cattle to feed the new mining towns.

Copper mining became very important in the late 1920s. New discoveries of copper were made at the time the metal was needed in the car and electrical industries in Europe and the USA. Zambia has depended on the export of copper ever since that time.

The cluster of copper mines and towns is shown on map (2). The area is called the Copperbelt. Three-quarters of the copper is mined underground and one-quarter comes from open pits. The type of mine and the date of opening is shown on the map.

Half of Zambia's 7 million people (1987) live within 40 kilometres of the railway. This means that most of the country, which is three times the size of the UK, is very thinly peopled. All the main towns are in the Copperbelt or along the railway.

2 Copperbelt

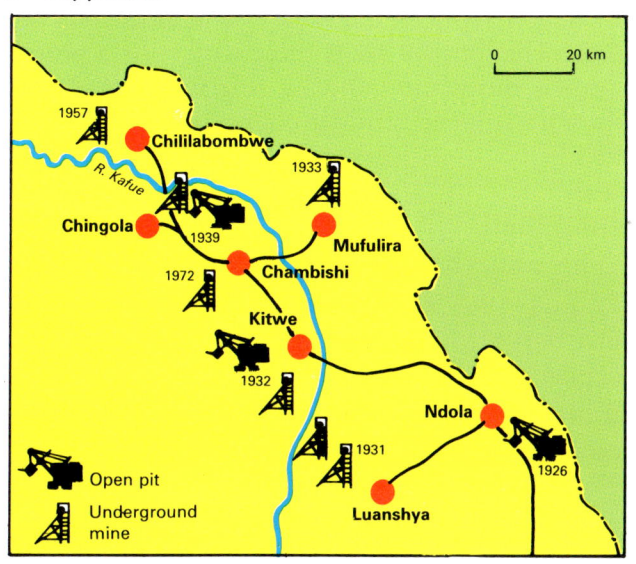

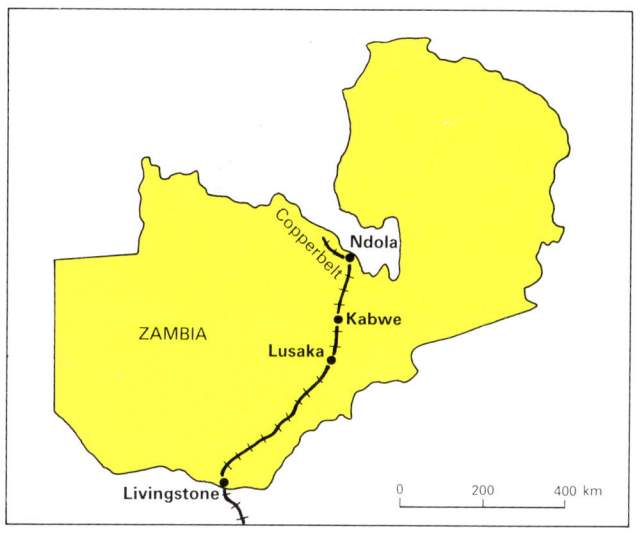

1 Zambia

Lusaka grew up at a railway sidings in 1905 to serve the Broken Hill mine. Today, it is the capital city with over half a million people. Kitwe is second city and the main mining and business centre on the Copperbelt. Ndola, the third largest city, is the distribution centre of the Copperbelt. Mufulira is the fourth largest city in Zambia with a population of 150 000 in 1981. It is the site of one of the largest underground mines in the world. You will find out about this mine by studying the photographs on pages 50 and 51.

Mine and township in the Copperbelt

THE RAILWAY GAME

The centre of southern Africa was a blank on the Europeans' map of Africa until the eighteenth century. In the period after 1870 railways were built to claim land and the minerals there.

In this game colonial powers build railways and open up the continent. Ask for details.

Routes to the coast

Zambia is a landlocked country in the centre of southern Africa surrounded by eight countries. This is a big problem for Zambia because her economy depends on the sale of copper to overseas countries. She also has to import bulk cargoes of wheat, coke, fertiliser and many other products from overseas. It would have been a great advantage to have a coastline or be near the sea. Routes to the coast are long and cross at least one other country. It is fortunate that there is a choice of routes to the coast because events in neighbouring countries may cause a route to close.

Study map (3) as you read about Zambia's many routes to the coast.

Tan-Zam railway

Main routes
Year: 1960
Route: to Beira by rail
Distance: 2330 kilometres
Advantages: A direct and reliable route. It was the only route used because of agreements made by the British colonial power to use Rhodesia (now Zimbabwe) railways and the port of Beira.
Problems: Rhodesia declared itself independent of Britain in 1965. This was an illegal act by the white government trying to prevent black Africans achieving majority rule. Zambia, independent since 1964, began to use other routes. This route has been used more since Zimbabwe became independent in 1980, but the line has been blown up by rebels many times.

Year: 1973
Route: to Lobito by rail
Distance: 2370 kilometres
Advantages: A direct route through Zaire and Angola, first used in 1965. Low freight charges. This was the chief route to the coast when the Beira route closed in 1973.
Problems: An outbreak of civil war in Angola in 1975 made the route unsafe. All traffic ceased.

Year: 1975
Route: to Dar es Salaam by road
Distance: 1715 kilometres
Advantages: In 1970 the Great North Road was tarred and a large fleet of trucks was brought into service. It is a short route and the journey often takes as little as five days. Freight costs are low. This became the main route when the Lobito route closed.
Problems: Competition from the new Tan-Zam (or Tazara) railway, increased price of petrol and poorly serviced trucks caused a decline in this route.

Year: 1977
Route: to Dar es Salaam by rail
Distance: 1860 kilometres
Advantages: The line was built by the Chinese at a low cost for the two friendly neighbours Zambia and Tanzania. It opened in 1975. It is a short route and freight costs are low. Most copper went by this route in 1977.
Problems: It is an unreliable route. The port of Dar es Salaam becomes blocked with traffic. The track has been damaged by heavy rain and by sabotage. Track maintenance is poor and there is a shortage of spare parts for trains and wagons. Lack of money to operate the line reduced traffic in 1985.

Year: 1985
Route: to East London by rail
Distance: 3464 kilometres
Advantages: It is a reliable route using South African trains and wagons. In 1985 70 per cent of copper exports went on this line.
Problems: This is the longest route to the coast. Freight charges on the railway and at the port are high. The journey takes three weeks. As a protest against the white minority rule in South Africa, Zambia stopped sending copper via this route in 1987.

Other routes
Other routes have been tried but soon abandoned.

Route 1: 1966, to Dar es Salaam by air
Five large transport planes were used to airlift copper to the coast. Route abandoned in 1969.

Route 2: 1966, to Dar es Salaam by road, ship and rail
The copper was carried by road to Mpulungu, across Lake Tanganyika to Kigoma and from there by rail to Dar es Salaam. Route abandoned in 1968.

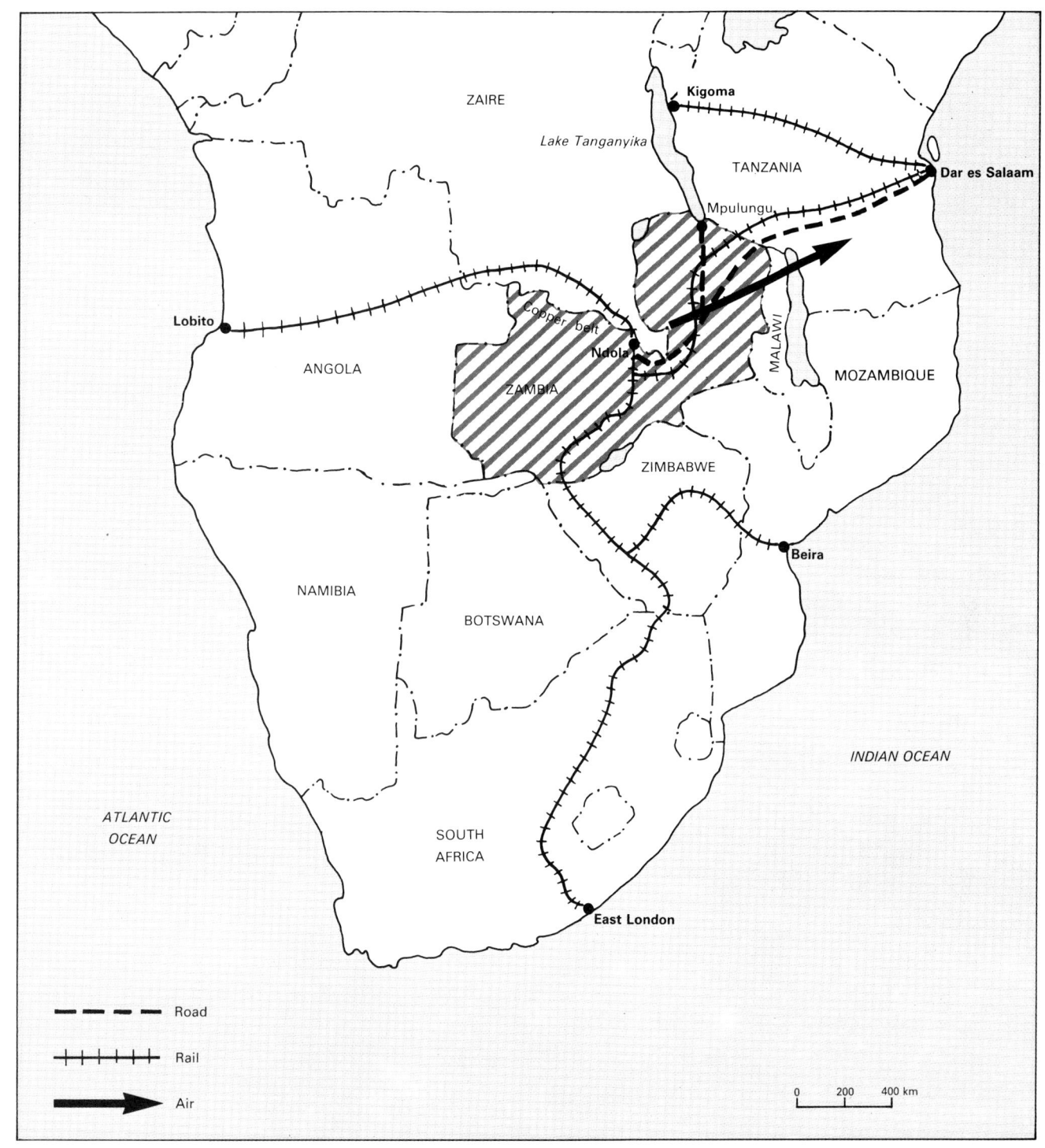

3 Copper routes

FOLLOW-UP WORK

1. Make a list of advantages which make a good route to the coast for large amounts of copper each year.
2. Make a list of the many reasons why routes have declined or closed.
3. Why does Zambia need more than one route to the coast?
4. Explain why many of Zambia's problems result from her landlocked location.

LANDLOCKED COUNTRY

A country which is surrounded by other countries. It has no coast and no ports. All imports and exports must pass through other countries.

A copper mine in Zambia

1 Mufulira mine is in the Copperbelt. This photograph shows the surface plant and some housing on the plateau surface 1250 metres above sea level and 13 degrees south of the Equator.

2 There are 9500 workers at the mine. They live with their families in the five townships. Each has brick housing, schools, clinics, piped water, electricity, paved roads, sewage disposal, youth clubs, sports and community centres.

3 There are five main shafts. Some are used to carry men and equipment; others bring out the copper ore and allow fresh air to circulate. The deepest shaft goes down 1000 metres.

4 The copper ore is an ancient sedimentary rock with 2 per cent copper content. Diesel-powered drills make holes for explosives which blast out a section of rock.

5 Mechanical loaders handle the rock underground. The caverns which remain after the ore is removed are called stopes. These are filled with sand and cement or are allowed to collapse.

6 Trains, shown here, and conveyor belts carry the ore along tunnels to a crusher station. The rock is broken up and hoisted by skip, 12 tonnes at a time, to the surface. Seven million tonnes are removed each year.

7 The ore is crushed to powder. This is mixed with water and the minerals float to the top (the concentrate). Smelting removes sulphur and iron, leaving copper which is cast into heavy blocks – anodes 99.80 per cent pure. These are taken to the refinery shown here.

8 The anodes are hung in dilute sulphuric acid next to pure sheets of copper – cathodes. An electric current breaks up the anode which is redeposited on the cathode shown here, 99.97 per cent pure. This is removed after 12 days, melted in a furnace and cast into bars; 140 000 tonnes a year.

A MODEL COPPER MINE

You can make a model which shows the surface and underground operations at a copper mine. It is based on the Mufulira mine. Ask for a model sheet.

(a) Colour the model using coloured pencils like this:
Granite rock – red
Metamorphic rock – purple
Copper ore (in the mining, crusher and storage areas) – green
Three types of sedimentary rocks (including the caved and mined-out areas) – orange, yellow, and brown

(b) Stick the model onto thin card to make it stronger. Cut around the outlines of the five pieces.

(c) Cut along the dotted lines of the largest piece with a craft knife. Bend this piece along the dashed lines to make a box. Secure the cross-shaded flaps inside the model with glue or adhesive tape.

(d) Cut along the dotted line of the waste tip piece. Pull one end in the direction of the arrow to the line a–b to make a cone. Secure with glue or tape. Bend the flaps downwards and slot them into the top of the model.

(e) Bend the refinery piece into a box shape. Slot the flaps into the top of the model.

(f) Slot the remaining two pieces into the top of the model. Sketch on the reverse side of these two pieces.

FOLLOW-UP WORK

Use your model to help you answer these questions.
1. Where was the copper ore first mined?
2. Why were the shafts and tunnels driven towards the copper ore through the granite rather than in the opposite direction through the sedimentary rocks?
3. Copper occurs in small particles in sedimentary rock. Earth movements in the past have folded the rocks which now dip deep into the Earth. Why does this make mining difficult?
4. When ore is mined out from an area the support pillars are blasted out and the overlying rocks collapse. In September 1970 a massive collapse of rock occurred without warning. A million tonnes of water, sand and mud rushed into the mine workings killing 89 men. How does the model help you to explain why this disaster could happen?
5. (a) Why did the site of buildings above ground have to be chosen with care?
   (b) Why is Mufulira a better site for buildings than most sites in Peru (see page 20)?

Mufulira mine

6. Bauxite from Brazil is processed in Canada (see page 43). Why is copper processed at the mine in Zambia and not in the country buying the copper?

7. (a) The mine opened in 1933. When do you think the mine will close?
   (b) Why is mining called a robber economy?
   (c) Draw bar graphs to show copper production in Zambia for each of the years shown in table (4). Use the vertical axis for production totals and the horizontal axis for the years. Use your graph to help you with question 7(d).
   (d) What is the main problem for a country, like Zambia, which depends for its future development on the sale of one mineral?

4 *Copper production in Zambia (1940–86)*

Year	Production (thousand tonnes)
1940	267
1950	281
1960	567
1970	684
1976	712
1980	610
1986	436

RESEARCH

Find out how igneous, sedimentary and metamorphic rocks were formed. Use your knowledge to explain why the metamorphic rock shown in the model lies between the igneous and sedimentary rocks.

Depending on copper

Zambia is the fifth largest producer and second largest exporter of copper in the world. Copper brings Zambia 85 per cent of all the money she earns in trade. This is a big problem because Zambia is at the mercy of industrial countries which buy the copper (5). A sudden drop in prices such as that in 1975 or the steady fall in prices in the 1980s (6) has meant that copper has been sold for less than the cost of production. Zambia has got into debt and there has been little money available for new roads, schools, hospitals or to help farmers grow more crops.

Most developing countries have the same problem. Developed countries, such as Britain, get cheap raw materials from developing countries. But developing countries pay high prices for manufactured goods from developed countries. With little or no profit from copper exports, Zambia cannot buy new mining equipment, spare parts, vehicles, oil, lubricants or other things she needs. The falling price of copper is one of many problems for the copper industry as you can see on the list which follows.

PROBLEMS OF THE COPPER INDUSTRY

1. Falling copper prices on the world market.
2. Falling demand for copper due mainly to the use of aluminium and plastics as substitutes for copper.
3. Competition from other countries such as Chile, the world's largest copper producer.
4. Resource depletion. Zambia's reserves of copper are dwindling.
5. Increased cost of mining. Deep mining is difficult and costly.
6. Low grade ores. The best ores have been used.
7. Falling output, due to ageing mining equipment.
8. Rising cost of transport to ports and markets.
9. Strikes halt production for many months.
10. Disasters such as at the Mufulira mine.

FOLLOW-UP WORK

1. Find a world map in your atlas. Ships loaded with copper take the shortest route to Britain. Will these ships use the Suez canal (7) if they sail from:
   (a) Dar es Salaam;
   (b) East London?

5 *Markets for Zambian copper (1985)*

Country	% of total exports
Japan	28
China	12
Italy	10
France	8
USA	7
India	5
UK	4
Others	26

6 *Copper prices*

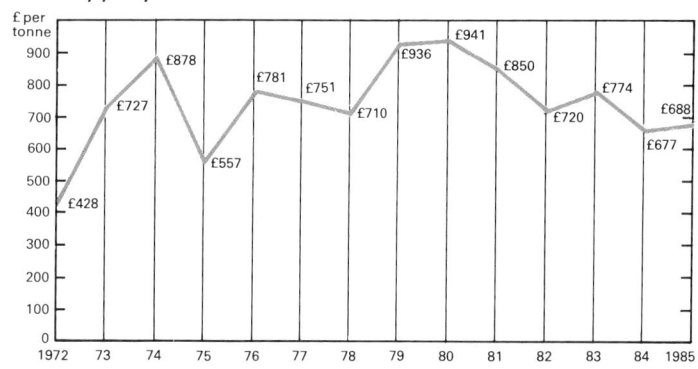

£ per tonne: 1972 £428, 1973 £727, 1974 £878, 1975 £557, 1976 £781, 1977 £751, 1978 £710, 1979 £936, 1980 £941, 1981 £850, 1982 £720, 1983 £774, 1984 £677, 1985 £688

2. The main markets for Zambia's copper are shown in table (5). Mark the sea routes from Dar es Salaam to each of those countries onto an outline map of the world. Show the amount of traffic by the thickness of the line drawn to scale. This is a flow-line map.
3. Study the list of problems of the copper industry. List them under two headings: NO SOLUTION and POSSIBLE SOLUTION. What conclusion do you come to concerning copper as the basis for the country's future development?

7 *Suez canal*

TOPIC FOR DISCUSSION

Developed and developing countries depend on each other. But the developed countries are rich and the developing countries are poor. They should work together to help each other.

A Zambian village

Lukali is a small village 10 kilometres north-west of Kapiri Mposhi. You can find Kapiri on a map of Zambia where the Tan-Zam railway joins the line from Lusaka to the Copperbelt. Lukali is not shown on the map because the site of the village has been changed many times. Sixty per cent of the population of Zambia live in villages similar to Lukali. The village is reached along a dirt road from Kapiri (8). This is savanna land with a mixture of tall grass, bushes and trees. The photograph was taken at the start of the dry season before the green vegetation had changed to a parched brown. Villages are built near to a water supply and you see two women from Lukali carrying water from a stream back to the village. The women spend many hours fetching water.

Lukali is a cluster of circular huts made from poles and mud with a thatched roof made from long savanna grass (9). The waterproof standard of the roof is put to the test in November when the wet season begins. Many of the roofs begin to steam at this time of year when the cooking is done inside the huts. The smoke from the fire helps to fumigate the roof and clear away some of the snakes and lizards.

8 The road to Lukali

There are 50 people in the village and they all belong to four families that are related to one another. One family includes father, who lives and works away from home, mother, grandfather and grandmother, mother's sister, the sister's husband who lives and works away from home, a 13-year-old son, an 8-year-old daughter, a 2-year-old son and a baby. There are separate huts for mother and father, the sister and husband, the grandparents and for the children when they grow up.

9 Huts in Lukali

Maize is the staple food. The cobs are kept in a basket grain store (10). This is built on stilts to stop mice and rats getting their share. A great deal of hard work is needed to make a stiff porridge called nshima. The grain is removed from the cobs by hand and put into a mortar with a small amount of water. It is pounded with a pestle for a few minutes to remove the outer coat of the grain (11). The broken grain is soaked in water for a few days and then pounded into flour. The flour is added to warm water and boiled over a charcoal fire for fifteen minutes. Nshima is also made from cassava flour prepared from the manioc root. The roots are not stored but lifted from the ground when they are needed. Nshima is eaten at mid-day and again at nightfall between 6.30 p.m. and 7.00 p.m. The nshima is put into a large bowl at the centre of the table, if there is one.

Nshima is always accompanied by a relish. This has one main ingredient which might be fish, chicken, goat's meat, beans, mushrooms, groundnuts or leafy vegetables. This is boiled with tomatoes, onions, red peppers, cooking oil, salt and sometimes curry powder. Some nshima is taken in the fingers, dipped in the relish and eaten. Kapenta relish is popular. Kapenta is a small fish of the herring family caught in Lake Tanganyika. It is dried in the sun and sold throughout Zambia.

Tea is the main drink taken with plenty of sugar and condensed milk. These items are bought at a shop along the road to Kapiri (12). The shop also sells beer, cigarettes, salt, soap powder and sacks of flour. Roller meal is a course flour machine-rolled from the whole grain. Breakfast meal is fine flour made from the inner part of the grain. The fine flour is mixed with water, sugar and tinned milk for breakfast.

10   The grain store

The main animals around the houses are dogs, chickens and goats. They scavenge for scraps, peelings and maize stalks and they are in a constant state of warfare with each other. Pigs are not kept. Oxen pull carts and are not used for meat.

11   Pounding maize grain

12   Roadside shop

Fruit is an important part of the diet. Oranges, bananas and papaws are grown in the village and wild fruit are collected from the bush. Insects add protein to a meal. The children catch flying ants, crickets and locusts. These are fried with caterpillars to make a tasty snack. The children have catapults and they are constantly shying at frogs, lizards and small birds which are then added to the relish. Hunting was once important in the dry season. Today, game laws limit hunting to small wild animals which the children bring home.

Soils around the village are poor but there is plenty of land to use. In the dry season, branches are cut from the trees over eight hectares of land. The branches are piled up on the soil where crops will be grown. The villagers burn the wood before the rains begin and the ash is turned into the soil with a hoe. The fire helps to clear the land and destroy any diseases in the soil. The heavy work is done by the men unless they work in the town. If women do this work less land is cultivated. After one or two crops the soil is exhausted and a fresh area of land is cleared and cultivated. This is a type of shifting cultivation Bemba-speaking people call chitemene ('cut over land') cultivation.

A FARM CALENDAR

You can make a calendar which shows the work that is done during the year in Lukali. You will see there is a close link between farming and the weather. You will discover that there is a wet season, dry season and hungry season. Ask for the calendar discs.

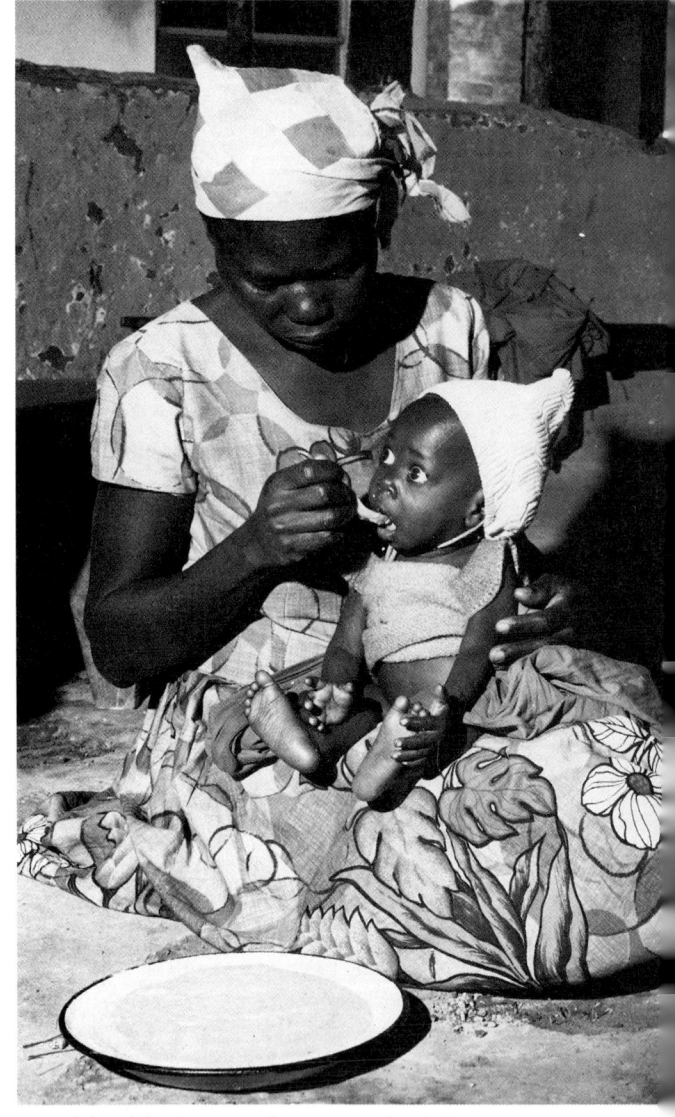

14 A healthy baby eating a protein-rich porridge

FOLLOW-UP WORK

1. How does chitemene cultivation help to explain why the village has changed sites many times?
2. (a) Draw a bar graph to show the monthly rainfall totals for Lukali. Use the figures in table (13), and a scale of 20 mm rain to 1 cm on the vertical axis.
   (b) Does rainfall come during the hottest or coolest part of the year? Explain your answer.
3. Study the farm calendar.
   (a) Why are branches cut from the trees many weeks before they are set on fire?
   (b) Why is the wood burned in October?
   (c) Why are crops planted in November?
   (d) What is the hungry season?
   (e) Why is the hungry season in February and March?
   (f) Why are maize cobs dried on the stalks for many weeks before harvesting?
   (g) Which crop is harvested when it is needed rather than at a fixed time of the year?
   (h) Why do you need to water late vegetables?
   (i) Why is it better to grow a variety of crops instead of one crop?

13 Rainfall statistics for Lukali

Total rainfall: 1125 mm

	Nov	Dec	Jan	Feb	Mar	Apr	May	Jun	Jul	Aug	Sept	Oct
Rain mm	120	250	300	230	180	30	4	0	0	0	1	10

Growing up in Lukali

Life is hard in Lukali from the day a baby is born. Babies are not given a name for three months because there is a fifty-fifty chance they will die and a name will have been wasted. The main reasons babies die are poor food and dirty water. A little education for the mother and the help of a clinic will give the baby a better chance of survival (14). But most women are not educated and they feed their babies with powdered milk mixed in dirty water. Many babies get diarrhoea, cannot eat and die. The baby which survives spends the first two years on the mother's back. It is safer here than on the floor amongst the kerosene drums and open fires. It is the best place to keep the baby when mother is clearing land, pounding grain, carrying water from the stream and cooking meals. When a new baby arrives, the young one is moved off the mother's back onto the floor where it fends for itself.

There are no toys to play with except those the children make themselves from wire and bottle tops. The children spend their time chasing around the compound (15) and hunting in the bush. There are jobs to do in the village such as pounding the grain and weeding the fields.

There is a school in a village 8 kilometres from Lukali. The boys usually get a place when they are seven years old and they stay until they are thirteen. Education is thought less important for girls but they might get a place when they are eight. It is a long walk to school and they often stay at home. The children are often ill. Lack of sanitation causes disease. The children relieve themselves in the maize field and urinate around the huts. Most children have hookworms in their stomachs. The eggs pass out of the body, hatch in the soil and the larvae bore through the bare feet of the next victim. Bilharzia is a disease caused by small flat worms which swell up the bladder and intestine. The eggs pass out with the urine, hatch out in water and breed in water snails. The snails pass out a fork-tailed borer which bores into the feet and legs of any child standing in an infected puddle, pond or stream. The bite of a mosquito causes malaria. Children who have malaria usually die when they catch another disease such as measles. The average length of life in the village is 45 years for men and 48 years for women. Children grow up fast in Lukali and soon have the job of looking after their parents.

PRIMARY HEALTH CARE

A system of health care which includes simple cures and methods to prevent diseases. A large number of rural clinics are set up. Village health workers are trained to give vaccine shots and cures for common ailments. They also tell people what causes ill-health and how to prevent it happening.

Ask for the exercise sheet on Africa.

---

15 *Children playing in the compound*

A YEAR OF DECISIONS IN LUKALI

Many issues have arisen during the year. Imagine that you are helping to make decisions for the family. Study each of the matters which follow and write about your decisions.

1. It is late November and the rains have not come. Should the maize crop be planted in the hope rain will soon arrive or should they wait until it rains? If the rains are delayed the maize crop will have to be planted again but the arrival of rain will mean an earlier harvest.
2. The town of Kapiri needs food. Should the family grow tomatoes and vegetables to sell in the town or use their land to grow crops for their own needs?
3. Father has returned home having done a seasonal job on a sugar estate (page 62). He has money to spend. There is enough money to buy three small items or one large item. Which items should they buy? Give your reasons.

   Small items A metal-framed bed and blankets instead of a grass mat, a bicycle, cigarettes and beer, clothing for all the family, sacks of grain, fertilisers and insecticides.

   Large items A brick house with tin roof and a window, a generator to make electricity, a milling machine for pounding grain (16).

17 *Dam across a stream*

4. The dry season has been very long. A small dam could be built across the stream (17) using boulders. This would save water to use in the home and in the fields. Some people say it will bring disease. Should a dam be built near Lukali?
5. The children have been treated for bilharzia at a clinic near their school. They have had injections to kill the parasites in their blood. What precautions must be taken in the village to stop the children catching bilharzia again?
6. Uncle has been offered a job in the Copperbelt. If he goes, the whole family of ten will go with him. They have to decide whether the future lies in the town (see page 59) or in Lukali. What do you think the family should do? Give your reasons.

16 *Using a milling machine*

Lusaka: capital city of Zambia

Lusaka was established in 1905 at a passing-point siding on the single-track railway between Livingstone and the Copperbelt. It was only a small settlement when – because of its central location – it was chosen as the capital of the British colony of Northern Rhodesia in 1935. The new government buildings, offices and low-density housing for Europeans were built on the cool and breezy Ridgeway (18). High-density housing was built to the south and west of Ridgeway for Africans who were government workers, cooks and servants. Administration and business were the main functions of the capital with some manufacturing to meet the needs of the European settlers.

When the country became independent in 1964 the earlier controls over the movement of Africans into Lusaka came to an end. The growth of the city since then is shown in table (19). When people first see the tall buildings rising from the plateau (20) they feel there must be a chance for a better life in the city than in their own village.

The city centre is on Cairo Road which is part of the Great North Road (21). There are office blocks, banks, department stores, cafés, restaurants, hotels, cinemas, a bus station and market. The factory area is on a branch line west of the main track. Factories process farm products from the surrounding area. The main products are cigarettes, beer, flour, vegetable oil, dairy products and farm machinery.

19 Population of Lusaka

Year	Population
1963	123 000
1969	238 000
1976	400 000
1981	559 000
1986	600 000

20 View across Lusaka

18 Plan of Lusaka

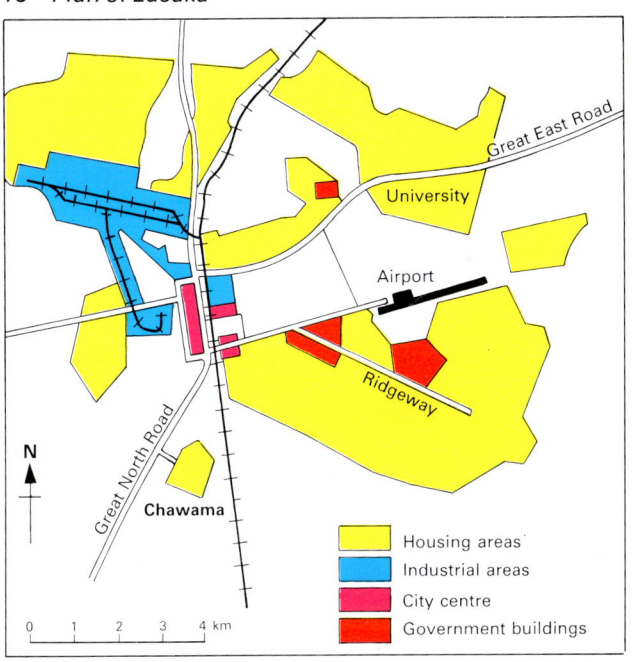

21 Cairo Road, the commercial centre of Lusaka

People coming from the countryside without skills and unable to read and write will find a job is hard to get. A large number of people work for the city council cleaning drains, mending roads, tending gardens and repairing public buildings. Boys may find jobs as houseboys, learn to cook, and later become waiters. Girls can find work as cooks and servants. Some people start little enterprises such as mending bicycles and selling food in the market. If one member of the family can find a job, their future in the city is more secure.

Most newcomers live on the outskirts of the city. If there is wood and grass available they will build a village-type hut (22) but these materials are in short supply and they often use packing case wood for the walls and beaten-out petrol drums for the roof.

When a family has become settled and father has found a job, they will build a better house on a compound controlled by the local council. The photograph (23) is the compound on the south of Lusaka called Chawama. The houses are made from sun-dried bricks. It is often said that the iron- and clay-rich soils of Zambia are better for making

22 Old-type houses in Chawam

INFORMAL SECTOR WORK

Self-employment in small-scale enterprises such as hawking and bicycle mending. It is not registered employment and gives a poor, irregular income. It is the only work for most newcomers to cities in the developing world.

SITE AND SERVICE SCHEMES

A method of controlled settlement used in Lusaka since independence to house large numbers of newcomers to the city. The authorities choose a well-drained site, lay out roads, mark out house plots, provide piped water, sewage disposal, street lighting and other community services. The families, often working together, build the houses. The authority provides a loan for the building materials.

There are also uncontrolled squatter settlements that the authority has improved with roads and services.

23 New houses in Chawama

24 Making bricks

25 Collecting water from the standpipe

bricks than growing crops. The soil is mixed with water, placed in a mould (24) and dried in the sun. Sheets of corrugated iron are nailed to planks to make the roof. There are small shuttered windows and a wooden door. A two-roomed house is home for the whole family. One room is the bedroom and the other is the living room. The cooking is done outside on a charcoal fire. Sanitation is a hole in the ground surrounded with a grass shelter for privacy. Chawama was built where there was good drainage which allows the sewage to filter away without causing diseases.

There is plenty of clean water in Chawama. A pipeline carries water from the Kafue river south of Lusaka. There are two taps on each standpipe which are close to the houses (25). If people are careless and allow large puddles to form around the standpipe there is a danger of catching malaria and bilharzia.

Maize grain made into nshima is the main food in Chawama. Father brings home a sack of roller meal on his bicycle each month. This does not provide all the vitamins and minerals that children need and the relish is often missing. A relish can be made from kapenta bought in the market, from chickens kept around the houses and from bone meat and offal from the city slaughterhouses.

The children do not have the chance of the extra snacks they had in the village. If there is enough money the family can buy tea, sugar, margarine, salt, cooking oil, tinned and powdered milk and even fresh milk. In this crowded community there is little chance of growing vegetables or tending a few fruit trees.

If the children are ill they join the long queue for the clinic. People who are very ill go to the city hospital.

There are schools in Chawama but there are not enough places for all the children. The lucky ones start at seven years old but many wait an extra year or more before they start. Parents hope their children will do well at primary school, pass the examination to go to secondary school and perhaps go on to university. Their dream will be that one son will get a job in government and the whole family will live in a big house on the east side of the track.

FOLLOW-UP WORK

1 Study the plan of Lusaka (18) and using your knowledge of the city suggest reasons why:
   (a) this city has government buildings and a university;
   (b) the city centre is well placed;
   (c) the best houses are on Ridgeway;
   (d) newcomers live on the outskirts of the city;
   (e) factories are located on the west side of the railway track.

2 (a) Compare life in Chawama with life in Lukali. Write your notes under the following headings: Houses   Water supply   Food   Sanitation   Health   Education   Work   Community life   Future prospects
   (b) Which place do you think offers the better way of life? Give your reasons.
   (c) Suggest some reasons why site and service settlements are better than uncontrolled squatter settlements.

3 (a) Why do you think old people often stay behind in the village when the young people move to the city?
   (b) What problems will there be for the old people remaining in the village?
   (c) Why do parents who have found work in the city want their parents to live with them?

Crops for sale

Most Zambians grow crops to feed themselves. This is called subsistence farming. There are a few large farms along the railway line which grow crops for sale. This is called commercial farming (26). These farms were set up by European farmers. When Zambia became independent, most European farmers left the country and most farms are now owned by Zambians.

Crops which are grown for sale are called cash crops. Most farms grow one crop which is usually maize, cotton, tobacco, groundnuts or sugar cane. These crops grow well in Zambia's tropical climate. The success of these farms depends upon the use of irrigation water. One successful project is the Nakambala sugar cane estate (27). The first cane was planted in 1964 between the Kafue river and the town of Mazabuka (population 10 000). By 1981, 10 000 hectares of land provided all the sugar Zambia needed.

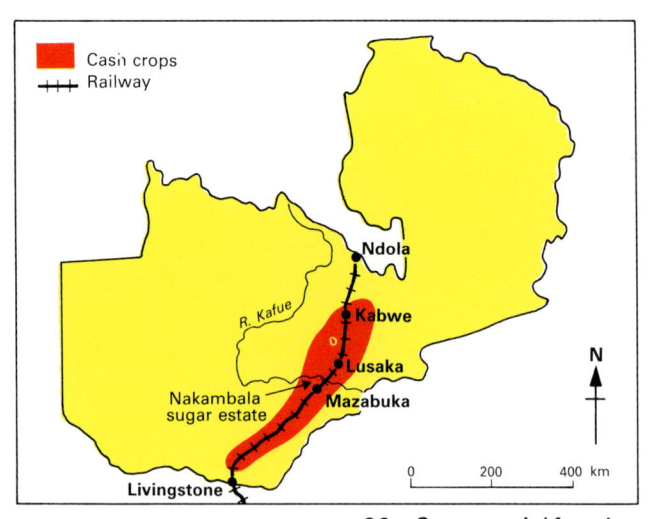

26 Commercial farming

Ripe sugar cane is harvested when it is twelve months old and three to four metres high. Three varieties are grown which mature early, in the middle of or late in the dry season (April to

27 The Nakambala sugar cane estate

October). Before it is cut, the crop is burnt to remove dead leaves and weeds. The cane is cut by hand and stacked in five-tonne bundles. One man makes one bundle each day. Tractors and trailers haul the cane to the factory. The cane is crushed to squeeze out the sweet juice. This is boiled to remove water and to form crystals of raw sugar. The triangular-shaped building in photograph (27) is the raw sugar store.

When the sugar cane has been cut, fertiliser and water are spread on the field and the plant grows again. Six or seven crops can be harvested before fresh seed-cane is planted.

From planting to cutting, the sugar cane needs 2000 mm of water. One-third of this comes from rainfall and the rest is taken to the fields by pipeline and canal. This is called irrigation. Each field is irrigated 20 times during the year. In the hot season the fields are irrigated once each week and during the cool season once every two weeks. Study the layout of the estate (28) and notice the position of the pipes and canals.

Water is taken from the Kafue river. A constant supply of water is certain throughout the year because the flow of water in the river is controlled by dams for the Kafue hydro-electric power station nearby. Twenty kilometres of pipeline carry water from the river to night storage dams. The dams are filled every night and the fields are irrigated during the day. Two hundred and fifty kilometres of canals carry water to the fields. The cost of irrigation is 15 per cent of the total cost of growing, harvesting and transporting the cane. The higher the irrigation water has to be pumped, the greater the cost of growing the crop.

There are 45 000 people on the estate. They live in traditional village houses or brick houses in six townships. Each town has shops and social clubs, a cinema, football pitch, a school and clinic. A training centre gives instruction on driving, engineering and office work. There is piped water, electricity and sewage disposal.

In the harvesting season, 1500 cane cutters work on the estate. They live there in barrack-type buildings and go home to their families at the end of the cutting season.

28 *Plan of sugar cane estate*

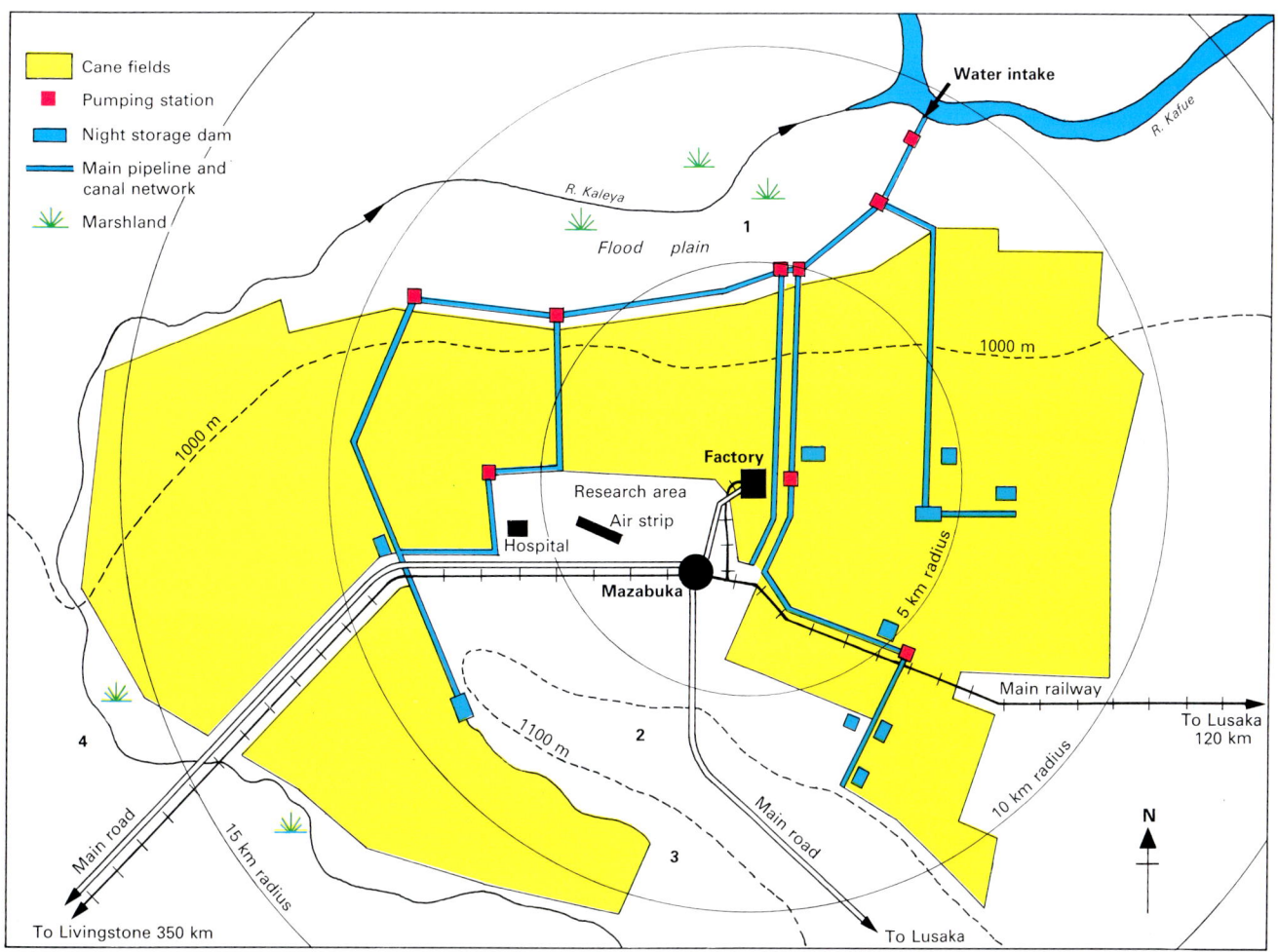

A farming future for Zambia

When Zambia's copper runs out at the turn of the century, farming may be the only means of earning money. The Nakambala sugar estate shows how this might be done but it is a costly operation using large amounts of water, fertiliser and equipment.

At present there are only 850 commercial farmers with more than 40 hectares of farmland. There are 380 000 subsistence farmers. Their inputs, apart from labour, are few and output is hardly enough to feed themselves. In some years there might be a little surplus to sell (29) if there is a town nearby. There is plenty of good farmland. Only 5 per cent of the best land is cultivated. There is water for irrigation and cheap supplies of electricity. There are also many problems.

PROBLEMS OF FARMING

1. The subsistence farmers have no claim on the land they farm.
2. They are shifting cultivators. Settled farming would cause the soil to lose its fertility, soil erosion would occur and crop yields fall.
3. Droughts are common and crop losses often great.
4. Transport is poor. Farmers might produce crops for sale which rot before they are collected.
5. One-quarter of the present cash crop harvest is lost owing to bad handling.
6. The government is slow to pay for crops. Farmers may not be paid in time to buy fresh seed and fertiliser.
7. Prices are often low to provide cheap food for the towns. Export prices might also be as uncertain as those for copper at present. Young people leave farms for jobs in cities if profits are low.
8. The cost of inputs such as fertilisers and machinery is high. Parts and fuel are very difficult to get.
9. Farmers often smuggle crops into neighbouring states to get a good price. This does not help Zambia.
10. Collective farming is often encouraged with farmers working in teams and marketing their crops together. Most farmers do not trust the system.

FOLLOW-UP WORK

1. Study maps (26) and (28). What advantages will there be for each of these locations:

29 Surplus maize for the city market

   (a) the sugar estate between the river Kafue and the town of Mazabuka;
   (b) the factory at the centre of the estate?
2. What advantages and problems will there be in having such a large area of land under one crop?
3. Briefly say whether the family in Lukali (page 54) would have a better life in a town on the sugar estate.
4. Study the farm calendar for the months April to October (page 56). Why does the family in Lukali suffer when father works as a seasonal cane cutter?
5. The factory made 110 000 tonnes of raw sugar in 1980. Extra land is needed to raise production to 150 000 tonnes. Areas 1, 2, 3 and 4 on map (28) can be used for cane growing. Which **two** sites would you use? Give your reasons.
6. Compare the Nakambala project with the Majes project in Peru (page 16). Which project do you think is the best for the country and for the people living there? Give your reasons.
7. Farming may be the foundation for Zambia's future development. Suggest how each of the problems of farming can be tackled to make this possible.

30 Victoria Falls

Power and industry

Zambia takes her name from the Zambezi river which flows through the country on its way to the Indian Ocean. Photograph (30) shows the river in the wet season crashing over the 106 metre rock face of Victoria Falls into the gorge below. The power of the river is used to make electricity near to the falls and further downstream in the Kariba gorge. Kariba dam (31) is 128 metres high, 617 metres across and carries a 12 metre wide road. It holds back a lake which is 282 kilometres long and 32 kilometres at its widest point. The dam was built in 1960 and there are power stations on both sides of the border in Zambia and Zimbabwe. There is another large power station on the Kafue river which is a tributary of the Zambezi. Find these rivers in your atlas.

31 *Kariba dam*

Three-quarters of the electricity from these power stations is used to refine copper in the Copperbelt towns (page 47). Zambia needs new industries because she depends too much on copper mining. Table (32) shows some of the factories already built and table (33) shows some of the factories she may build.

32 *Location of factories*

Location	Product	Details
Ndola	Petrol and chemicals	There is an oil pipeline between Dar es Salaam and Ndola. Oil refinery opened in 1973.
Luanshya	Copper wire and cable	The factory converts local copper into a high-value product.
Kafue	Textiles	Local cotton is made into cloth.
Kafue	Fertiliser	Nitrogen fertilisers are made using large amounts of electricity.
Lusaka	Cigarettes	International tobacco companies use local tobacco to make cigarettes to sell in Zambia.
Livingstone	Cars	Five thousand cars a year are assembled from kits imported from Italy.

33 *New factories for Zambia*

Cement	Iron and steel
Lorries and buses	Bicycles
Maize grinding machines	Televisions
Air conditioners	Farm tools
Furniture	Clothing and shoes

FOLLOW-UP WORK

1 What advantages are there for producing hydro-electric power in Zambia?
2 Which two industries from table (32) are of least value for Zambia's development? Give your reasons.
3 Zambia has little money to spend on new factories. Select five factories from table (33) which you think will be of most value for Zambia's development in the next few years. Give reasons for your decisions.
4 Does manufacturing industry, farming, or a combination of these offer the best future basis for Zambia's economy? Give your reasons.

Wildlife: the struggle for survival

The savanna grasslands of Zambia support a rich variety of wild animals. Elephants, buffaloes, zebras, giraffes, antelopes and rhinoceroses are herbivores and eat plants. Carnivores such as lions, leopards and cheetahs eat meat. Finally, there are scavengers who feed on what the carnivores leave. Study photograph (34) which shows many links in a food chain which includes grass, zebra, lion and vulture.

Adult elephants and rhinos are herbivores but they are not attacked by carnivores. They are very large, powerful and they use their tusks and horns as weapons. The main enemy of these animals is man. Rhinos are killed for their horns. In 1971 there were 67 000 rhinos in Zambia and in 1981 there were only 15 000. The poachers are villagers who are expert hunters. They saw off the horns and pass these to dealers. The horns are used for dagger handles in the Middle East or are powdered and used as a medicine in the Far East.

There are now laws which stop most people hunting animals for meat. National parks have also been set up to protect wildlife. Map (35) shows the two main parks. Over 60 000 people visit these areas every year to see and photograph the animals.

The national parks are infested with tsetse fly which spread disease to cattle. The wild animals are naturally immune to this disease. Villagers can only get meat by hunting but they risk being sent to prison if they are caught. The Poaching Game deals with the struggle for survival in a national park. Ask for the game sheets.

34 Animals of the savanna

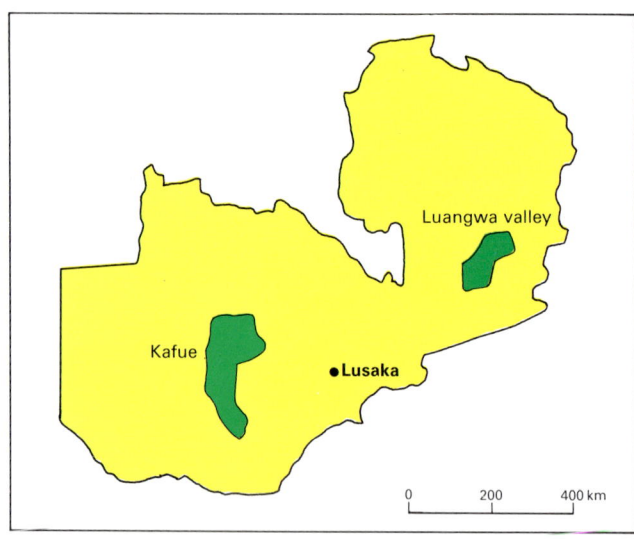

35 Wildlife parks

36 Elephants in the dry season

FOLLOW-UP WORK

1 Describe the food chain shown in photograph (34).
2 Use your knowledge from the game to say why:
   (a) elephants travel great distances during the year;
   (b) the number of elephants in a park must be controlled;
   (c) national parks are needed to save the black rhino from extinction;
   (d) poachers have a great deal of success.
3 The number of black rhinos is getting less each year. Suggest ways to stop the decline in their numbers.

TOPIC FOR DISCUSSION

The lives of people in traditional hunting villages are more important than the need to preserve wild animals or the pleasure of tourists visiting national parks.

India

Contrasting landscapes

India is the seventh largest country in the world (1). In its total land area of three million square kilometres there are three contrasting landscapes (2). In the north, three parallel ranges of the Himalayan mountains over 6000 metres high form a natural wall between India and the centre of Asia (3). South of the mountains, the valleys of the Indus, Ganges and Brahmaputra rivers form an alluvial plain which is flat land covered with silt left by the rivers when they flood (4). The southern part of India is a plateau called the Deccan at about 600 metres (5). The plateau slopes eastwards from a mountain range called the Western Ghats. The rivers rise in these mountains near the west coast and cross the plateau to the east coast on the Bay of Bengal. The Eastern Ghats are hills forming the eastern edge of the Deccan.

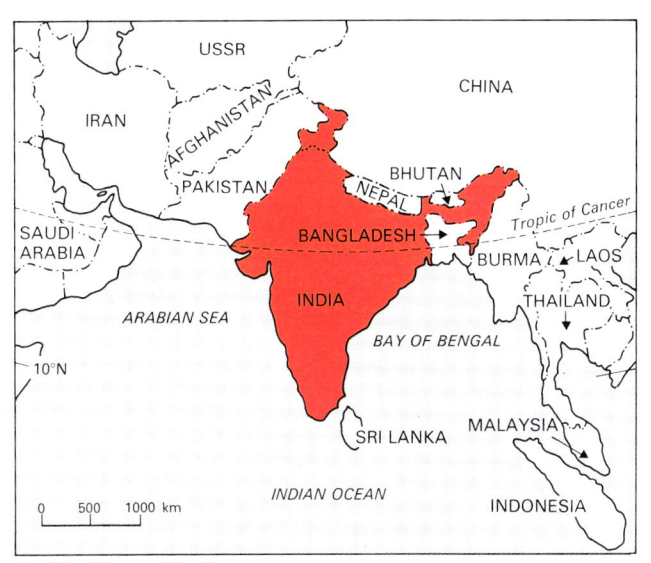

1   Position of India

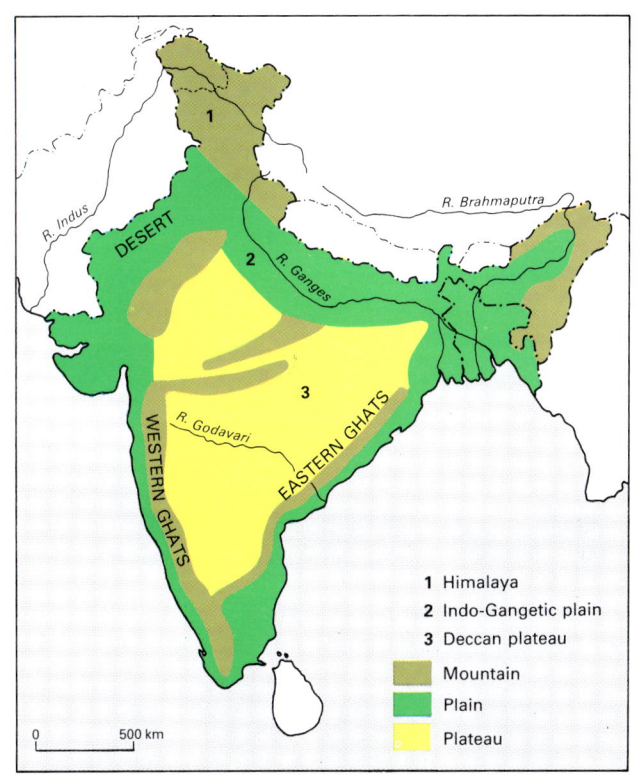

3   The Himalayas

Farming on the Ganges plain

2   Landscapes of India

5   On the Deccan

67

A problem of people

India has the second largest population in the world after China. In 1987 there were 800 million Indians and each year the number is increasing by 2 per cent. At this rate there will be 1000 million people in India by the year 2001. Study the statistics in table (6) which show the growth of India's population this century.

6 Population of India

Year	Population in millions
1901	241
1921	251
1941	320
1961	439
1981	684
2001	1000

The number of children born each year is more than the people who die. Better medical care, improved hygiene and more reliable supplies of food and water mean that fewer children die and that people are living longer (7). Indians generally have large families and although the government encourages people to have fewer children, this change is taking place slowly, as is shown in table (7).

7 Birth and death rates

Year	Birth rate (per thousand people)	Death rate (per thousand people)	Average length of life (years)
1911	48	44	25
1961	41	19	45
1971	37	15	49
1981	35	15	50
1987	33	12	54
UK (1987)	13	12	74

8 Family planning poster

Many improvements are being made in farming (see page 74) to produce more food. Extra food helps to feed the extra millions each year, but there is little surplus to give people enough food to live a healthy life. The rapid growth of population is the main reason most Indians live in poverty. When people do not have enough food to eat and their diet lacks minerals and vitamins, they do not have the strength for work and suffer many diseases. Beriberi, kwashiorkor, rickets and night blindness are very common, especially in children (9).

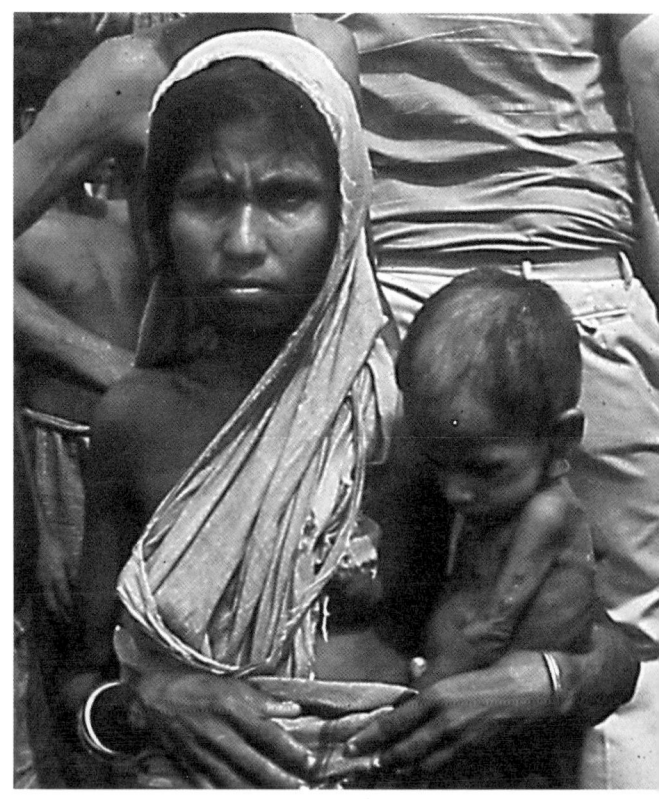

9 The very poor suffer from malnutrition

VICIOUS CIRCLES

Millions of people are trapped in what are called vicious circles where one unfortunate fact of life leads to another. How can the circles be broken?

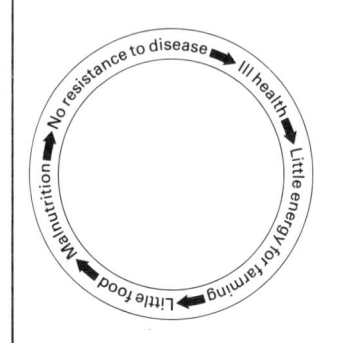

Malnutrition → No resistance to disease → Ill health → Little energy for farming → Little food → Malnutrition

Poor tools and seeds; no fertilisers → Low yields → No savings → Little money → Poor tools and seeds; no fertilisers

Feeding the people

Every year there are millions of extra people to feed. With a high birth rate and low death rate the population rose by 116 million between 1981 and 1987 (6). This is more than double the number of people who live in the UK. Seventy per cent of Indians live in the countryside and work on the land. One hundred and eighty million people scratch a bare subsistence from less than 0.2 hectares and another 140 million are landless labourers. Map (10) shows where most people live and map (11) shows the crops that they grow.

Rice gives more food value per hectare than any other crop and is grown wherever a hot and wet climate allows. A lot of the work in the fields is done by hand. Transplanting rice seedlings into a flooded paddy field is a back-breaking job (12). Wheat is grown in drier, cooler areas or follows rice in the drier, cooler part of the year. Photograph (13) shows women making chapattis from wheat flour. Millet is grown where it is too dry for rice and wheat.

Religion influences what people eat. Eighty-three per cent of Indians are Hindus. They do not eat meat. There are 183 million head of cattle in the country, the largest number in any country in the world. They mainly work in the fields and provide some milk. Pork is not allowed in the diet of Muslims, who make up 11 per cent of the population. People who live near the sea eat fish and sea food. The main source of protein is milk.

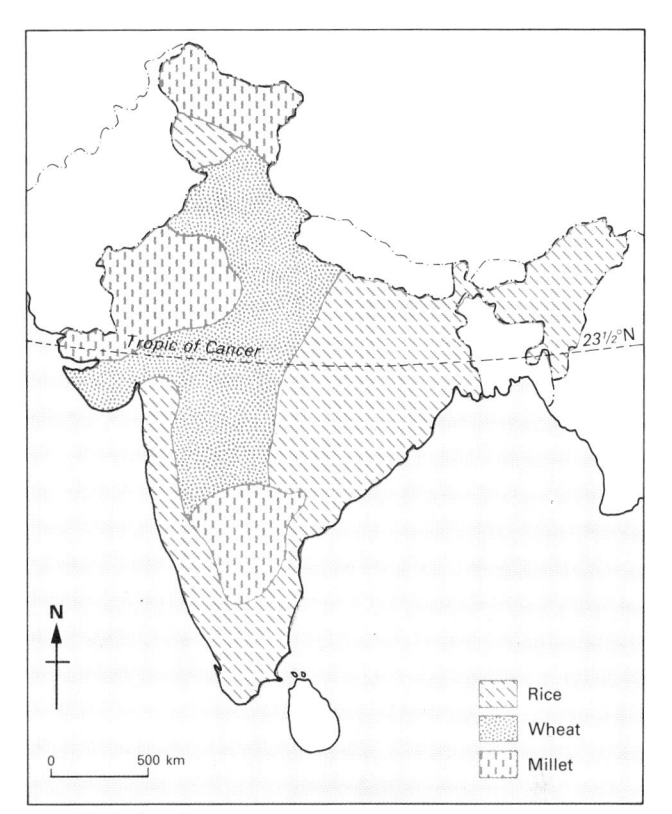

11 Main food crops

10 Where people live

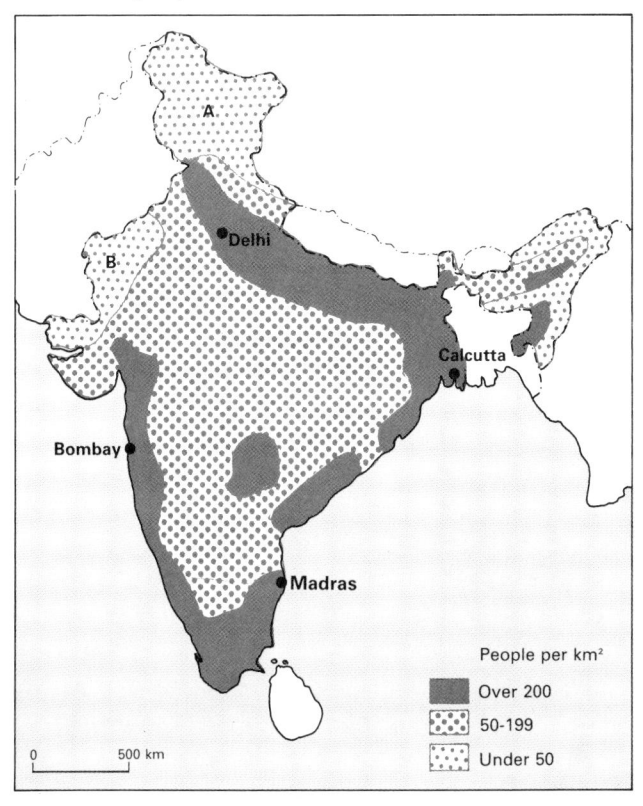

12 Transplanting rice

13 Making chapattis

FOLLOW-UP WORK

1. It is 1000 kilometres along the length of Britain from Land's End to John O'Groats. How many times would Britain fit along the length of India? Take your measurement from map (2).
2. Study maps (2), (10) and (30).
   (a) Why do large numbers of people live near to the coast and on the Indo-Gangetic plain?
   (b) Why do few people live in areas A and B shown on map (10)?
3. Draw a line graph to show the growth of population in India from 1901 to 2001. Use the statistics from table (6). Use a scale of 100 million people to 1 cm of the vertical axis.
4. (a) What does the graph show about the rate of population growth:
      (i) between 1901 and 1941;
      (ii) between 1941 and 2001?
   (b) If the population is still rising at the rate of 2 per cent a year in 2001, what will the population of India be in 2002?
5. Study the statistics in table (7).
   (a) What change must occur in the birth rate to stop the growth of population?
   (b) Why has the death rate fallen at a faster rate than the birth rate in India?
6. Study map (11).
   (a) How much of India lies south of the Tropic of Cancer?
   (b) Why is the diet of people in south and east India different from that of people in north-west India?
   (c) Which of the two photographs (12) and (13) was taken in north-west India and which in southern India? Explain your answer.

THE DEMOGRAPHIC TRANSITION

The process of change in the population structure of a country. During the change the population rises rapidly. (Ask for more details.)

Poverty in the countryside

Half of all the people living in poverty in the world live in India and the neighbouring country Bangladesh (1). Between 1941 and 1981 the population more than doubled in size (6) and the number of people living in poverty also doubled. Too many people to feed brings hunger which leads to sickness, malnutrition and early death. Babies born in India will live 20 years less than those born in Britain (7).

Most people live on the land and use traditional methods of farming which have not changed for hundreds of years (14). Life is hard and most families are at the mercy of the weather. The crops need rain but this does not always come (15).

There are many more reasons why people live in poverty in the villages of India, as you will see when you read about life in just one of these.

14 Traditional farming methods

15 A year without rain

70

A village in India

The village is on the Deccan plateau 100 kilometres from Nagpur and 600 kilometres from Bombay (30). A dirt track joins a highway 10 kilometres from the village. This is the only link to a nearby market town and distant city.

There are a thousand people in the village. They live in mud houses which have roofs of straw (16). Most houses have two rooms. The main room is about 8 square metres and is used for eating, sleeping, entertaining and doing craftwork. The other room is the kitchen. Heavy rain in summer wears away the walls and seeps through the roof.

Electricity came to the village five years ago but few people use it because they cannot afford to buy the meter.

The soils are thin and stony. They are baked hard by the sun, leached by summer rain (see page 41) and exhausted from centuries of use. The main crops are wheat, cotton, vegetables and groundnuts. A few cows and goats are kept.

17 Picking cotton

16 Houses in the village

This is a very dry area for eight months of the year. India gets most rain in summer when winds blow off the sea onto the land (30). This is called the monsoon. The village is a long way from the sea and it is much drier than the coast. There is usually rain between June and September but the amount of rain varies from year to year. Two years of plentiful rain are often followed by a drought. Many years ago, an earth dam was built across a small stream near the village. This collects some of the rain in summer to make a small reservoir. This is called a tank. The water is used for drinking and to irrigate the nearby fields (19). When the rainy season has ended the small lake quickly disappears. The water has either been used, evaporated or soaked into the ground. Hand-dug wells near the tank provide water in the dry months. Water is pulled to the surface by women and girls using a bucket at the end of a rope.

18 Primary school

A few villagers are tradesmen such as the cobbler and tailor but most are farmers. Men, women and girls work long hours in the fields. Half of the land is owned by three landlords who live in Nagpur. Some people are tenant farmers and give 40 per cent of the crops to the landlord as rent. Others earn two or three rupees a day weeding the wheat and picking cotton (17). (18 rupees = £1 in 1987.) When there is no work there is no money. Young men sometimes help in the fields but many look for jobs in the offices or cotton factories in Bombay where they earn much more money than from farming.

There is a village primary school (18). There are no chairs or desks and classes are large. Learning is done by repeating the words from a text-book many times over. Most girls spend only two years at school. At eight or nine most girls can earn a little money working in the fields or looking after the baby while mother is at work.

The villagers are Hindus and belong to social groups called castes. These groups are based mainly on money and jobs. Children belong to the same caste as their parents. Marriages are arranged between people in the same caste. There are many people in the village without land who do the hardest and dirtiest jobs like sweeping the street and carrying away the sewage. They are called Harijans which means 'children of God', which replaced the old term 'untouchables'. They live in one-roomed huts at the edge of the village and use their own well.

Traditional ways of life, including the caste system, make it very hard for any changes to take place in the village.

The village has been chosen for study by a government team of scientists. Their aim is to find ways of improving life for poor people in the village. Their first job was to study many families. The Das family was one of these.

Ram Das was born in the village 44 years ago. He owns two hectares of land which he took over from his father when he died. He never went to school but he learnt a great deal from his parents and from the village radio. He filled in chart (20) which tells us about his family and the problems of village life. Study the details carefully.

19 Ram Das leads water to one of his fields. His daughter has brought his food and collects water for the home

The village council, the Panchayat, has five members including Ram Das. It will meet to discuss the ideas of the government team of scientists. The council will decide how best to use the money given by the government to improve life in the village. They will then have the job of organising the villagers to do all the work that is needed.

20 Ram Das' questionnaire

Family	Head of family	Age	Occupation
Das	Ram	44	Farmer

Other members of family in household	Wife 40; son 21; son 17; daughter 13; daughter-in-law 20; daughter-in-law 17; grandson 3; grandson 1.
Other members not in household	Son 19 (office worker - Bombay); son (dead - cholera); daughter (dead - typhoid)

House type	Rooms	Walls	Roof	Veranda	Courtyard
Single storey	4	Mud	straw	✓	✓

Nearest healthy drinking water	Sewage disposal
2 kms	Pit in courtyard

Possessions	Jewellery; charpoys (string beds); built-in, mud brick stove; storage jars; cooking utensils; shrine; picture of the Hindu god Khrishna; farm tools. Animals - 2 bullocks, 1 cow, 6 goats

Land	Owned or rented	Size	Number of fields	Together or separate	Average distance from house
	Owned	2 hectares	5	Separate	2 kms

Irrigated	Method used	When used
2 fields	Ditches from tank	3 months after rains

Crops grown	Wheat, vegetables, cotton, groundnuts

Main daily tasks	Average time taken per day
Farming	3 people × 9 hours
Travel to fields	3 people × 1 hour
Watering and pasturing animals	1 person × 8 hours
Collecting firewood	2 people × 2 hours
Fetching water	3 people × 1½ hours
Cooking, washing, cleaning.	3 people × 4½ hours

Family's major problems	
	1/ Land area too small to support family and make money
	2/ Lack of water and poor soil produce low yields
	3/ Amount of time spent on daily tasks such as water and firewood collection.
	4/ Money owed to moneylender at high rate of interest.
	5/ Lack of protein in diet leads to weakness and ill health - children not developing correctly.
	6/ Lack of education as all of the family need to work full time.
	7/ House leaks badly in rainy season.

FOLLOW-UP WORK

1 Work in small groups. Discuss each of the ideas A to K put forward by the government team of scientists. You have 150 units to spend. Decide how to spend the money and write about the decisions you make.

A Tube wells

Wells can be drilled, like an oil well, to draw water from a greater depth than a hand-dug well. The water is clean and free of salt. It is good for drinking and irrigation. The well for drinking water can be sited at the edge of the village (21).
Cost. Tube well with hand pump for drinking water   20 units
Tube well with diesel or electric pump for irrigation water   50 units

B Larger tank

The present small tank can be dug deeper and wider. This will allow more water to be stored in the rainy season. The villagers will have to be organised into work teams (22) and paid for the work they do.
Cost. For labour in money or food   30 units

C Biogas

Methane gas is given off when cattle dung is fermented in a pit (23). 150 cattle make one tonne of dung each day. This amount will make enough gas for every stove in the village. There will also be gas remaining to power a generator to make electricity to pump water and for three hours' light each night. The sludge is rich in nitrogen and is a good fertiliser.
Cost.   20 units

21 Tube well with hand pump

22 Digging the tank

23 Biogas unit

D Irrigation pipes

Pipes can be laid in trenches to carry water from the tank to all the fields in the village. At present only fields near the tank are irrigated.
Cost. For pipe and labour to dig trenches   20 units

E Polythene sheeting

Tanks and irrigation ditches can be lined with large sheets of polythene to cut down on the loss of water by percolation into the soil. The sheeting can also be used to line the roofs of houses.
Cost.   10 units

24 Poultry rearing

F Poultry
The scientific breeding and rearing of poultry (24) will bring a steady profit and a better diet for all the villagers.
Cost. For poultry stock and wire   10 units

G New seeds and fertiliser
Hybrid seeds including Mexican dwarf wheat will give high yields if there is a plentiful supply of fertiliser and water.
Cost. For one year's supply of seed and chemical fertiliser   20 units

H Grain silos
Twenty per cent of the harvested grain is lost each year because of poor storage. The grain spoils and rodents and other creatures take their share. Metal grain silos (25) preserve the grain until it is needed.
Cost. To supply the village   30 units

26 Tractor and trailer

25 Grain silo

I Tractor and trailer
Deep ploughing can be done if there is a tractor in the village. The top few inches of soil is, at present, exhausted of nutrients. The tractor will speed up the preparation of the land between crops if there is enough water stored to grow two crops in one year. Much of the carrying work can be done using the trailer (26).
Cost.   50 units

J Threshing machine
One threshing machine will do the work for the whole village. It will replace the traditional hand methods.
Cost.   20 units

K Co-operative
Farmers working together can raise money to buy seed, fertiliser and new tools. The whole village could be one co-operative. The farmers would no longer be in the grip of the money lender who asks high rates of interest. Surplus produce can be marketed together. A warehouse and truck are needed.
Cost.   50 units

27 Children learn to weave at the craft workshop

2 (a) Which of your new developments, if any, will help to solve each of the major problems for Ram Das listed 1 to 7 on chart (20)?
  (b) What advantages will there be for Ram Das if the council could re-distribute the farmland so that his land was in one field and not in scattered plots? (This is called land consolidation.)
  (c) Why will the council find this a difficult task to achieve?
3 The council owns some land. Money earned from farming this land is used to help the village. Over the next ten years the council has decided to use this money for the following projects:
  A New primary school with more teachers
  B Health clinic including family planning
  C A television room
  D Craft workshop for weaving cloth (27)
  E Surfacing the link road to the highway
  (a) In which order do you think the projects should be done?
  (b) What advantages will there be for the village from each of the five projects?

APPROPRIATE TECHNOLOGY

The use of simple machinery and equipment which the villagers can operate, maintain and afford. It is appropriate to their needs.

Drought, flood and disaster

The winter months in India are dry. North-east trade winds blow off the land towards the Indian Ocean (28). Air over the warm ocean expands and rises forming a low pressure area (less weight of air). Falling air over northern India forms a high pressure area. Air flows across the surface of the

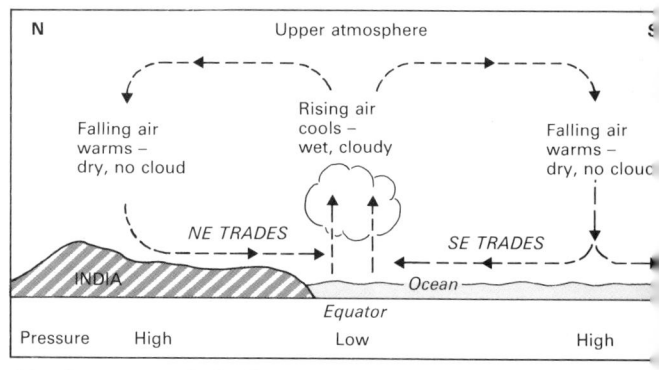

28 Dry season in India

Earth from the high pressure area towards the low pressure area.

Early in the summer it becomes very hot. A reporter in Delhi writing at the end of April gives an impression of what the heat is like.

'The temperature is 39 °C and it will rise to 44 °C next month and in June. The land burns like hot metal. Nowhere in India is the heat more intense. Even night brings no relief. People stay up late because it is too hot to sleep and dawn is the opening of a furnace door, a punch in the face. People suffer from heat exhaustion and sometimes die from it.'

Tanks dry up and the earth cracks (29).

The monsoon

The air over India is now hotter than the air over the Indian Ocean. Hot rising air over the north of the country forms a low pressure area and moist air is drawn towards it from the ocean. This is the south-west monsoon (30).

The wind reaches Bombay about June 5th, moves at about 20 kilometres an hour reaching Calcutta about June 15th. The wind is deflected up the Ganges valley by the Himalayas arriving in Delhi about July 1st. The rain comes in downpours (31) and continues into September. The coming of the monsoon rain brings the temperature down a little. But the dry heat is replaced by sticky, humid heat.

29 Cracked earth in a drought

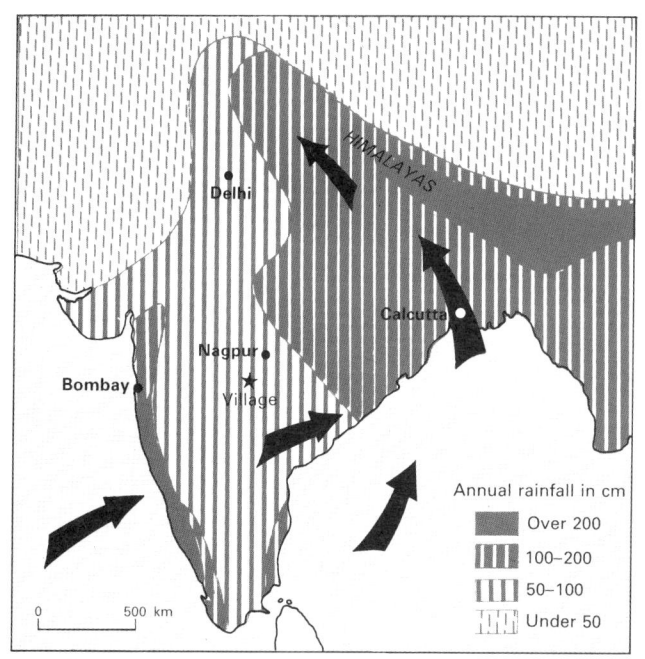

30 South-west monsoon

31 Sheltering from monsoon rain

32 Floods in Calcutta

The river Ganges, fed by heavy rain and melting snow from the Himalayas, floods across its plain. In September 1980, 43 000 villages were submerged by the floodwater, over a million homes were damaged and 1600 people were killed. The streets of Calcutta were knee-deep in water (32).

In 1987, the monsoon failed to arrive in north-west India. Much of the Deccan which is in the rainshadow of the Western Ghats had no rainfall. Crops died and wells dried up. The woman in photograph (33) is digging into the bed of a river for water to drink.

In the past a summer drought has brought famine. In 1943, more than three million people died from hunger when the monsoon failed to bring rain. Since then dams have been built to store water. Large amounts of food are produced in north-west India using irrigation water from the Indus, high yielding seeds, fertilisers and machinery. A reserve of food is stored to use in any year when rain-fed crops over most of India wither away in a drought.

33 Digging with bare hands for water

THE GREEN REVOLUTION

The increase in food production around the world made possible by using high-yielding varieties of wheat, rice and other grain crops. The success of these crops depends upon the controlled use of irrigation water, and heavy use of fertiliser and pesticide.

The new varieties of crops have been used in India since 1966. The wheat-growing areas of the Punjab were the first to use the new seeds and methods. Fragmented farms were consolidated into sizeable areas, irrigation was provided from new wells and river control schemes, co-operatives set up and machinery used (34). The methods have since spread to a wider area (35). These new developments have brought advantages and problems.

Advantages

- Food production has increased by 3 per cent per year which is ahead of the 2 per cent rise in population. Grain output rose from 50 million tonnes in 1950 to 150 million tonnes in 1986. The threat of starvation has declined.
- The government has surplus food to distribute to any area hit by drought or flood.
- Farming in many areas is modernised and well-managed with community water and pest control programmes.
- Two crops of fast-growing new varieties extend employment over a longer period of the year for labourers.

Problems

- The new methods can only be used by better-off farmers. Small farmers with little land and no money do not benefit.
- Land becomes more valuable. Landowners raise rents and remove tenants to take all the benefits themselves. More people become landless.
- The government has helped the new developments but small landowners and people in the south have had little help.
- The use of machinery means fewer jobs.
- The cost of inputs raises food prices. Poorly paid labourers suffer. Poor people cannot afford to buy the surplus food when drought strikes.
- Irrigation has caused waterlogged and salty soils which may have to be abandoned.
- Clearing forest for cultivation plus the more intensive use of land is causing soil erosion.
- Large amounts of costly fertilisers have to be imported.
- The production of pesticides resulted in the Bhopal disaster (36).

34 Combine in Punjab

35 Canal link map

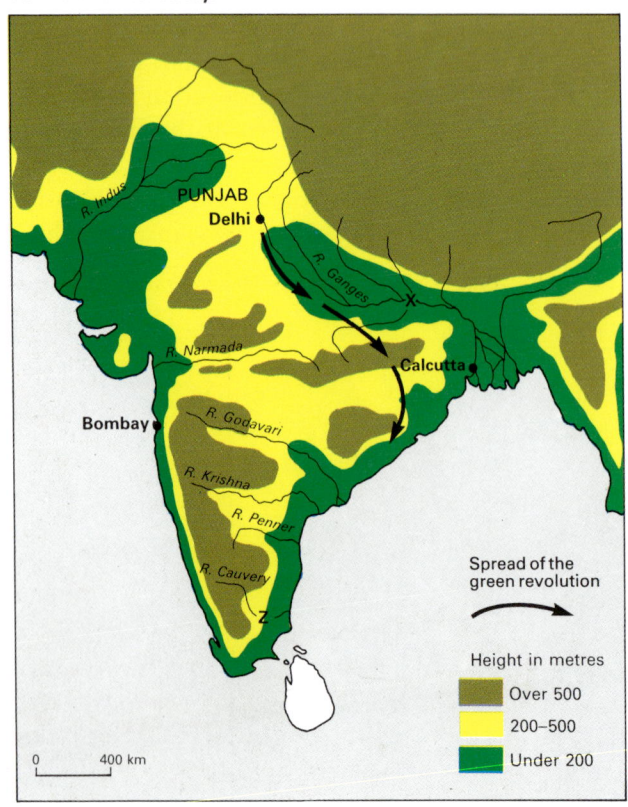

36 The Bhopal disaster

In the early hours of 3rd December 1984, as people slept in the city of Bhopal, poisonous gas leaked from a tank in a pesticide factory and spread across the city. More than 2500 people died. Ask for more details and discuss the issues raised by the disaster.

FOLLOW-UP WORK

1 Draw a bar graph to show the monthly amounts of rainfall in Bombay. Use the statistics in table (37) and a scale on the vertical axis of 1 cm to 50 mm.

37 Bombay average monthly rainfall (mm)

J	F	M	A	M	J	J	A	S	O	N	D
3	3	3	3	18	485	617	340	264	64	13	3

2 Study your graph.
  (a) Why is this a suitable climate for growing rice?
  (b) At which time of the year will irrigation water be needed most for the new crop varieties?
  (c) 'When the monsoon fails there is a drought.' Explain in full what this statement means.
3 (a) Compare the farming scene in photograph (34) with that in photograph (14) on page 70.
  (b) What are the advantages and problems of using mechanised farming in India?
4 Study the lists of advantages and problems of the green revolution.
  Do the problems outweigh the advantages?
  Discuss your opinions and write up your conclusions.
5 More land needs to be irrigated to increase food production on the Deccan. Most rivers flow from west to east across the country, carrying three-quarters of their precious water back into the sea (35). A canal could be built to carry surplus water from the Ganges to the dry lands of the south.
  (a) Copy map (35). Mark the route of a canal from the Ganges at X to the Cauvery at Z.
  (b) The canal would be 7 metres deep and 74 metres wide. Suggest as many uses as you can for the canal.
  (c) Why might the canal *not* be built?

Cities

Calcutta is the largest city in India and it has the most problems. It was founded in the late seventeenth century by the British East India Company as a port on the Hooghly river, the main arm of the Ganges to the sea (38). In 1858, Britain took over the rule of the Empire of India and Calcutta was capital city until 1912. It has remained a centre of commerce and grown into a large industrial city.

In 1946, when India became independent, Calcutta had three million people. By 1960 the number had doubled and by 1981 there were more than nine million living along a 40 kilometre stretch of the Hooghly river.

Most people have come from the surrounding countryside. Some are refugees who came from Bangladesh during the civil war which brought that

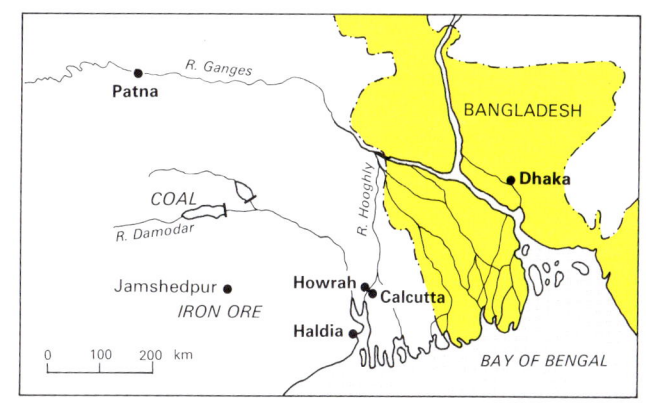

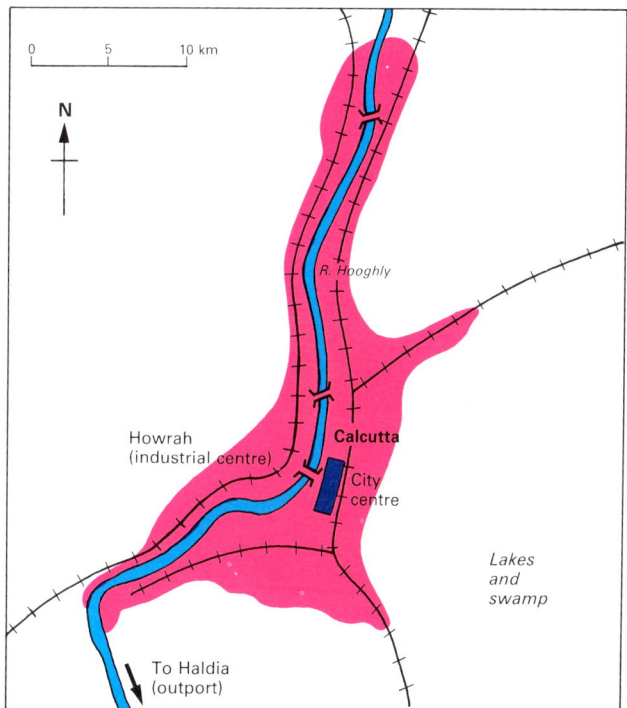

38 Calcutta: site and location

39 Calcutta's crowded streets

country independence in 1971. Added to this are the large number of babies born every year which makes Calcutta India's most overcrowded city.

The streets teem with people (39). A quarter of a million have no home at all and live on the streets. Three million live in shanty towns called bustees (40).

Bustees of Calcutta

The bustees are Calcutta's slum areas. Every city in India has them. The worst are collections of huts made from timber and corrugated iron. They are grouped around courtyards, each with an open pit for sanitation. Water comes from a tap in the alley and supplies more than one hundred people. Open drains run down the alleys. In the rainy season the drains overflow. Disease spreads quickly in these conditions. Tuberculosis (TB), cholera and leprosy are common.

Unlike slums in other countries, the bustees have been developed on private land. There is a three-tier system of ownership. There is a landowner who pays taxes to the city corporation, the hut owner who pays rent to the landowner and the hut dweller who pays rent to the hut owner. One-third of the population live in bustees like those in photograph (41). Seven families share this alley. Each family has one room in which to eat and sleep. There is some work at the local clock factory (42) but no school places for most of the children.

40 An improved bustee

Wealth and poverty exist side by side in the city (43). Half a million people have no homes and sleep on the pavements. Thousands more have comfortable homes with televisions, modern

41 An alley in a bustee

80

furniture and vehicles to get about the city. They own land and property, work in business, industry, transport and the professions. They shop in big stores in the city centre, visit museums and theatres and perhaps travel to and from work on the new underground railway.

Calcutta is a wealthy city. Industries process the farm products of West Bengal. There are jute mills, food and tobacco factories, cotton textile mills and engineering works. The port handles one-tenth of India's trade, and distribution trades employ 40 per cent of the working population. Banks in the city centre handle one-third of India's financial business, making the city a financial capital. It is also the capital city of West Bengal and thousands find work in administration and in ministerial offices.

The wealth of the city continues to attract thousands of migrants. Many come to escape the lower castes in the village. Most are young men who come in search of work. They scratch together a few rupees each week to send back to their families in the villages. If they get a better job they will bring the family to the city; otherwise they return home.

One-quarter of all Indians now live in towns and cities. This is more than 200 million people, which is the same number of people living in the USA and four times the number of people in the UK. There are 140 cities with more than 100 000 people and 12 of these have more than a million (44).

42   Industry in the bustee

43   Rich and poor in the city

FOLLOW-UP WORK

1. (a) Study map (38). Describe and give reasons for the shape of the city.
   (b) Why does the site of the city increase the problems of overcrowding?
2. (a) Describe the scene in photograph (41). Mention the uses for the alley, the houses and the number of people there.
   (b) Measure out an area 3 m by 3 m, which is the size of the one-roomed house. What problems will there be for a family of seven living there?
3. (a) Imagine your family has left a village in the Deccan (pages 71 and 72) to live in Calcutta. Write about the changes that have taken place in your life.
   (b) Why do people go to live in the city?
4. The worst slums are being knocked down and blocks of flats built in their place. Other bustees are being bought up by the planning authority and improved. In what ways can a bustee be improved?
5. (a) List all the reasons why people have moved into Calcutta in recent years.
   (b) Why are most migrants to the city men aged between 20 and 40?
6. Draw a sketch based on photograph (43). Write a paragraph about the hopes and realities which find expression in your sketch.
7. Study table (44). Is Calcutta a primate city like Lima in Peru and Lusaka in Zambia? Explain your answer.

44   Sizes of cities in millions (1981)

Calcutta	9.2
Bombay	8.2
Delhi	5.7
Madras	4.3
Bangalore	2.9
Hyderabad	2.5
Ahmadabad	2.5
Kanpur	1.7
Pune (Poona)	1.7
Nagpur	1.3
Lucknow	1.0
Jaipur	1.0

Industry

Under British rule, India supplied raw materials such as raw cotton and raw jute for Britain's factories and a market for Britain's manufactured goods such as cloth and metal products. The first new industries in India were jute mills in Calcutta in 1834 and cotton mills in Bombay in 1851. Textile industries grew quickly with exports going mainly to China.

Early this century, coal resources were developed and railways built. The first iron was made at Jamshedpur in 1911 (38). When India gained her independence, the country was no longer tied to the needs of Britain's economy. The new Indian government started a series of five year plans providing money to build new factories, open mines, construct power stations and develop transport and ports.

Basic industries came first with steel (45) and cement, for example. These were the materials needed by other industries such as machinery and construction.

India is rich in iron ore, bauxite, manganese, phosphates and many other minerals. These are

45 Iron and steel works at Jamshedpur

being developed. Coal, water and uranium are the main sources of power. Oil is in short supply but India produced 70 per cent of her own needs in 1986.

Agricultural raw materials are still the basis for India's most important industries. Cotton, jute, sugar and tea industries all depend on agriculture (46).

46 India's main industries (1982)

	% of industrial workers
Textiles	23
Food and drink	22
Metals	10
Machinery	9
Electricity	9
Chemicals	6
Transport equipment	5
Wood products	5
Mineral products	4
Others	7

New industries are being developed in fast-growing cities such as Bangalore and Poona. These industries include vehicles, machine tools, farm machinery (47) and electronics. Small industries are also coming to the villages of India. These products range from cotton cloth to components for assembly industries, such as televisions, in the cities.

Nuclear power stations, aircraft and space satellite industries (48) show that India can tackle the most advanced industrial projects. At the same time India struggles with the problems of the countryside and overcrowded cities.

47 Tractor assembly

FOLLOW-UP WORK

1. Study map (38). What advantages has Jamshedpur for an iron and steel industry?
2. India plans to build more steelworks, cement and fertiliser factories. Why do you think these are important industries for India?
3. Why do these *not* provide products for export?
4. Study map (48).
   (a) What are the two main forms of transport for India's industries?
   (b) Why is Bombay a good location for oil refineries?
   (c) Why is Visakhapatnam a good location for exporting iron ore to Japan?
   (d) Eighty per cent of India's coking coal for the steel industry comes from the Damodar valley (38) and the rest comes from Australia and Canada. Taking this into consideration and using the information on map (48), say why Visakhapatnam is a good location for India's first coastal steelworks in 1987/88.
5. Study the trade figures in tables (49) and (50).
   (a) Why has India searched widely for oil?
   (b) Why is there only a small range of exports?
   (c) Study the total values. Why is India said to have a poor balance of trade?
   (d) Why will India be less vulnerable to a recession in the world economy than countries such as Brazil and Malaysia which have developed export-oriented manufacturing industries?

48 Locations of major industries

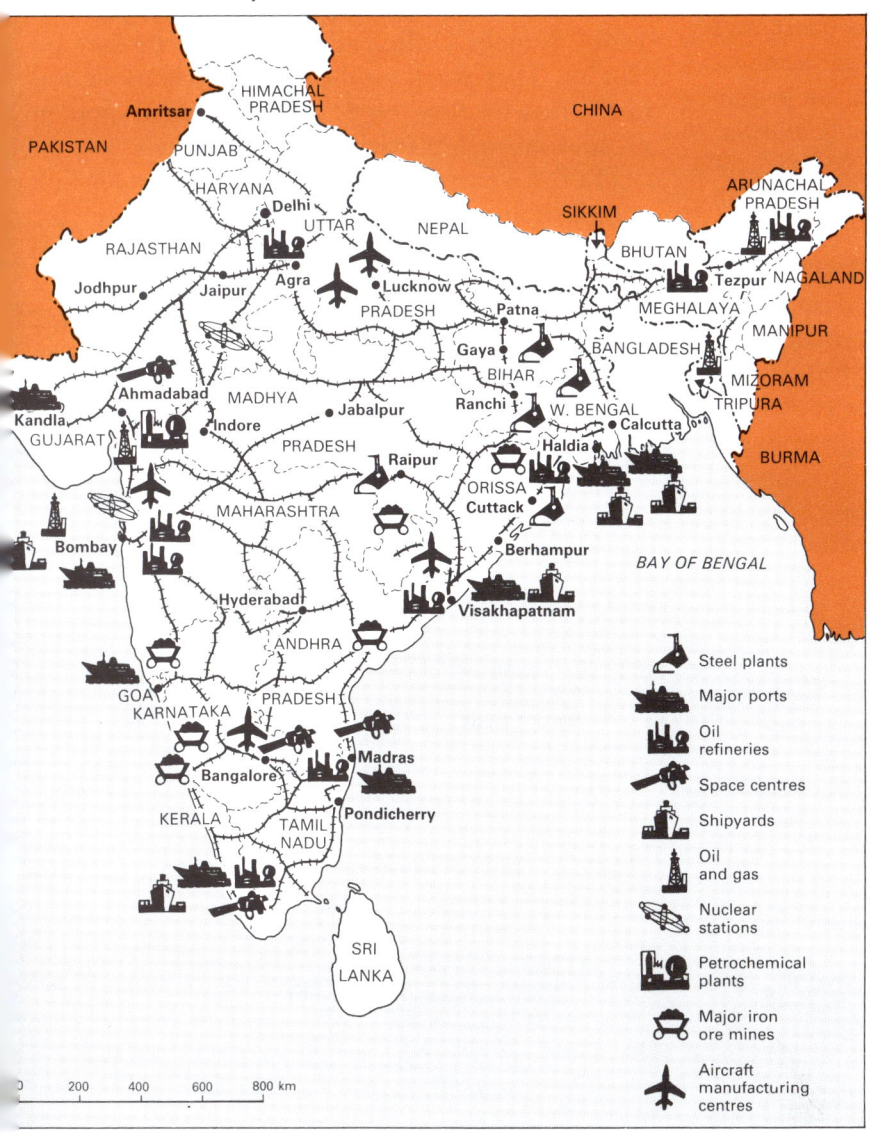

HEAVY INDUSTRY

The manufacture of bulky products. This includes the iron and steel industries and heavy engineering.
India has concentrated upon these industries as a basis for industrial growth and to save the cost of imports. These are called import-substitution industries.

49 India's major imports (1985)

Imports	Million rupees
Crude oil and products	53 820
Machinery and equipment	26 175
Fertilisers	8 620
Edible oils	8 302
Steel	7 773
Chemicals	7 691
Non-ferrous metals	3 451
Others	55 098
Total	170 921

50 India's major exports (1985)

Exports	Million rupees
Cotton textiles, garments	13 626
Gems and jewellery	11 946
Engineering goods	11 708
Tea	7 078
Iron ore	4 472
Leather products	4 252
Jute textiles	3 410
Fish	3 358
Others	56 719
Total	116 569

Malaysia

A mixture of peoples and places

Malaysia is a country in three parts. The peninsula of Malaya is separated from the states of Sabah and Sarawak, on the island of Borneo, by 600 kilometres of the South China Sea (1). Malaysia lies close to the Equator, and tropical rainforest covers 70 per cent of the country. There are mountains inland from the coast, and it has always been easier for the people living near the coast to contact each other by sea (2) than by land.

Until the nineteenth century, there were few people living in the area that is now Malaysia. Malays grew rice at places along the coast and native tribes lived in the forest and along the coast of Borneo. In 1987, there were 16 million people and 83 per cent of them lived on the peninsula. Forty-eight per cent of the people are Malays, 34 per cent Chinese and 9 per cent Indians. With the remainder belonging to other races you can see that Malaysia has a mixture of peoples and places.

The Chinese and Indians came to work in the tin mines and rubber plantations which were set up by the British in the nineteenth century. Tin mines were opened on the peninsula of Malaya in the 1850s and workers were brought from China. Roads, railways and ports were built and the tin exported to Europe. In 1910, the first rubber plantations were set up along the roads and railways and the workers were brought from India. Find Malaysia on a world map in your atlas. Notice the position of China and India. Chinese were also brought in large numbers to farm and develop the forests on the island of Borneo. Today, one-third of the people in Sarawak and Sabah are Chinese.

The Malays speak the Bahasa Malaysia language and their religion is Islam. They are the poorest

1 *Malaysia*

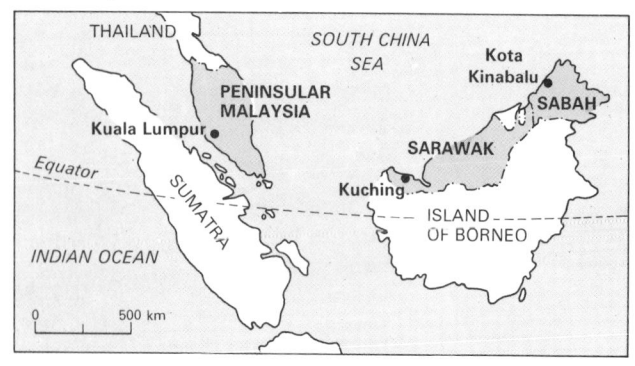

2 *Coastal settlement in Sabah*

people in Malaysia. Most Malays are farmers and fishermen who live in villages called kampongs (3). The Chinese speak the Hokkien or Cantonese dialect and they are Buddhists. They work in the tin mines and run most of the business and industry in the towns. The Indians speak languages such as Tamil, Punjabi, Urdu, and Hindustani and they are Hindus. They work on the rubber plantations and in the towns they work as shopkeepers and in professions such as teaching and the law.

The three parts of Malaysia share a common link with Britain. British protection of states on the Malay peninsula began in 1874 and in Sarawak and Sabah in 1888. Peninsular Malaya became independent in 1957. In 1963, Malaya, Singapore, Sarawak and Sabah joined together to form Malaysia. It was felt that one country would be stronger than the four separate parts. In 1965, the mainly Chinese community of Singapore decided to become an independent country leaving Peninsular Malaysia, Sarawak and Sabah as one country.

FOLLOW-UP WORK

1. Study map (1). What is the distance by air from the national capital Kuala Lumpur to:
   (a) Kuching, the state capital of Sarawak;
   (b) Kota Kinabalu, state capital of Sabah?
2. Explain how the following can help to unite the three parts of Malaysia:
   (a) sea and air transport;
   (b) television;
   (c) education in schools.
3. There are three main races of people in Malaysia.
   (a) What advantages might this have?
   (b) What problems might there be?
4. Explain how British colonialism brought about:
   (a) a country made up of separate places hundreds of kilometres apart;
   (b) a mixture of races;
   (c) an economy which depends on the export of raw materials to the developed world.

The Malays: poverty in the countryside

3 Kampong surrounded by paddy fields

The Malays are a race of people who came from the island of Sumatra to live on the peninsula of Malaya. They are known as the bumiputra which means 'sons of the soil'. They are rice farmers and fishermen.

Malay villages are called kampongs. There is a cluster of houses, a mosque and school set within a grove of coconut palms and fruit trees which give food and shade (3). The houses are made of wood with a steep roof made from corrugated iron. They are built on stilts because of the tropical heat, heavy rainfall, floods, rats, snakes and insect pests. Most kampongs are built near a river on flat land where paddy-rice can be grown. The fields surround the kampong and each farmer has three or four scattered plots which he either owns or rents from a landlord.

Tenant farmers pay rent to their landlord and when they have paid the miller and repaid some debts there is little money left. But they also pay a tax, called the zakat, to help people with no land and no food to eat. Those with the most money pay the most tax.

The Malays are poor. Malnutrition, disease and the death of young children are very common. You will find many reasons for the poverty of Malay farmers as you study one area on the west coast of the peninsula (4).

The land in the study area is flat with a large area of swamp. The clay soils are rich in nutrients but badly drained. Temperatures are always high, between 27 °C and 30 °C. Heavy rain is caused by the heat of the overhead sun and monsoon winds from over the sea (4).

4 Rice farming

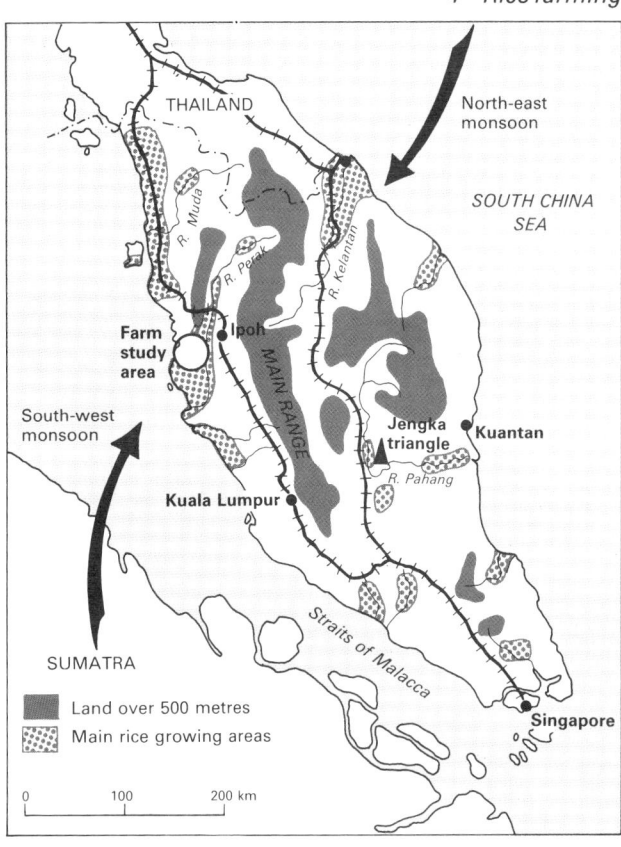

5 Experiments in the paddy fields

All the farmers in the study area are Malays. There are usually six or more people in a family. They are Muslims and religion is a way of life. The pace of living and work is slow. Most parents have had no education above the primary school. Seventy per cent of the children go to school between the ages of six and fifteen.

SUBSISTENCE FARMING

Producing food for the family or village community. A subsistence crop is the basic item of the diet which in the case of Malays is rice. Semi-subsistence farming is where most crops are for the family but some produce is for sale.

6 Threshing the rice

The average sized farm is one hectare. One crop of rice is grown each year. It is sown in July and harvested in January. The land is poorly prepared. A scythe is used to slash down the weeds which have grown since the last harvest. The field is harrowed with an iron rake pulled by a water buffalo. There are no machines.

There are not enough canals to control the flow of water to the fields and they are too deeply flooded. Seeds are sown in a nursery bed which is a floating platform of banana stems (3). It takes six weeks for the seedlings to grow long enough to be transplanted into the flooded fields. The farmers use their own poor seed from the previous harvest. No fertilisers are used. Sprays may be used if a crop has been attacked by pests and diseases. Rats, insects and disease destroy 20 per cent of the crop every year.

The crop is harvested by sickle and threshed into a tub (6). The grain is not dried but stored or sold as soon as it has been threshed. Half the rice is used to feed the family and the rest is sold to pay rents, debts and the zakat.

One way to help farmers in this area is to give them more land. This has been done by moving

7 Clearing the forest

some families from their farms. The farmers who stay are given three hectares of land in one field instead of scattered plots. Families moved from the area are re-settled further inland. The Jengka triangle (4) was the first of these schemes.

In 1956, gangs of men began to clear tropical rainforest alongside the Pahang river (7). The best timber was carried away on lorries (8). The other trees were burnt and the seedlings of oil palms and rubber trees were planted in the ashes (9). Roads, houses, clinics, schools, shops and mosques were built before the families arrived.

Each family was given a wooden house (10), four hectares of planted land and a small plot for vegetables, fruit trees, goats and poultry. The rice farmers had to be taught how to farm their new cash crops. The cost of the house, land and fertiliser had to be re-paid over 15 years from the sale of their palm oil and rubber. By 1987, 75 000 people were living in the Jengka triangle where 30 years earlier only a few aboriginal hunters had set foot.

8 Hauling away the logs

9 A field of young oil palms

COMMERCIAL FARMING

Producing food for sale rather than for the direct use of the grower. In the Jengka triangle this includes cash crops such as oil palm.

---

10 Malay family house

FOLLOW-UP WORK

1. Study map (4).
   - (a) Why are rice farms near rivers?
   - (b) Why does the south-west monsoon (June–September) bring more rain than the north-east monsoon (December–March)?
   - (c) Which monsoon is blowing during the rice-growing season?
2. Explain why each of the following **helps** the farmer:
   - (a) clay soils;
   - (b) flat land;
   - (c) high temperatures;
   - (d) heavy rainfall;
   - (e) a large family.
3. Explain why each of the following is a **problem** for the farmer:
   - (a) a one-hectare farm;
   - (b) scattered plots of land;
   - (c) growing one crop each year;
   - (d) zakat;
   - (e) a large family.
4. What can be done to solve the problem of:
   - (a) swampland;
   - (b) deep water in the fields;
   - (c) poor yields (see photograph (5));
   - (d) pests and diseases;
   - (e) wet grain rotting in the store?
5. How can twice the amount of grain be produced from the same fields in one year?
6. Study map (4). Suggest why the Jengka triangle was chosen as the location for this scheme.
7. Study the plan of the Jengka triangle (11).
   - (a) You set off by car from Kuala Kerau and travel round the triangle at 60 km/h. How long will the journey take?
   - (b) Give reasons for each of the following features of the plan:
     - (i) forest has **not** been cleared from the top of the hills;
     - (ii) rubber trees were planted in different areas from the oil palms;
     - (iii) the route of the main road through the triangle;
     - (iv) where the villages were built.
8. Make a copy of map (11). Mark onto your map a good location for each of these developments:
   - (a) a town in the triangle;
   - (b) a plywood factory (12);
   - (c) a palm oil processing factory;
   - (d) a rubber processing factory.

   Give reasons for your decisions.
9. Study photograph (8). Explain how the removal of forest may bring short-term benefits but long-term problems to these highland areas.
10. Explain how the Jengka triangle scheme might benefit the settlers and the people who remain in the villages but not the aboriginal tribes of the forest.
11. Why is the integrated rural development scheme in Malaysia likely to be more successful than settlement schemes in the Amazon forest (page 40)?

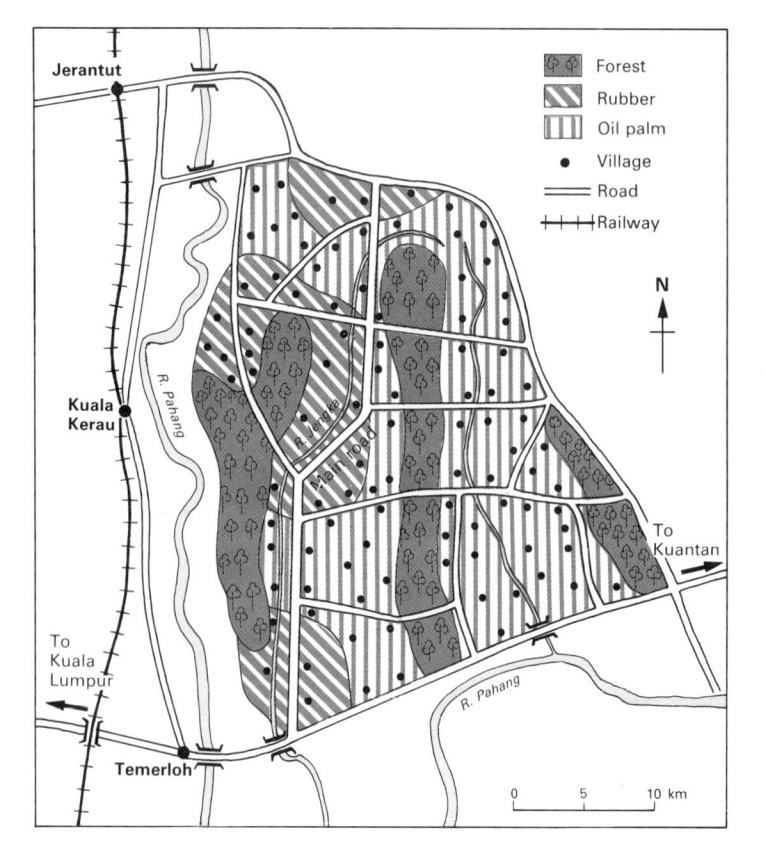

INTEGRATED RURAL DEVELOPMENT SCHEME

A scheme which combines clearing the forest, planting main crops, building villages, selecting and placing settlers, managing the project, providing credit, setting up processing (12) and marketing facilities and aiding community development. The Jengka triangle was the first scheme and model for 300 others. They are planned and undertaken by a government agency called the Federal Land Development Authority (FELDA).

◀ 11 *The Jengka triangle*

12 *Plywood factory*

Tin

The Main Range is formed from the rock called granite which contains lodes of tin (see page 20). Over many thousands of years the granite has been worn down by rivers. Gravels containing tin are now spread on the surrounding plains (13). The gravels on the west side of the Main Range have most tin and the Kinta valley is the largest tinfield in the world. The tin has been mined since the fifteenth century but modern mining started in the 1850s.

The Malays would not leave their rice farms to work in the mines and Chinese had to be brought from south China to provide the labour-force. Roads, and later railways, were built from the ports to the mining areas to bring food and equipment to the mines and to take out the tin. Mining villages sprang up on the tinfields and these have grown into large towns and cities such as Kuala Lumpur and Ipoh.

One method of mining tin is by dredging. Huge dredges floating on pools of water dig up the gravels containing tin from swamplands (14). The tin is removed from the gravels on the dredge and the waste is dumped at the back of the pool.

Tin is also mined using high-powered hoses called monitors (15). A jet of water breaks away the gravel from the mine face. The tin-bearing gravel now in water is pumped up to wooden sluice boxes called palongs. The heavy particles of tin are trapped behind slats of wood in the sluice boxes

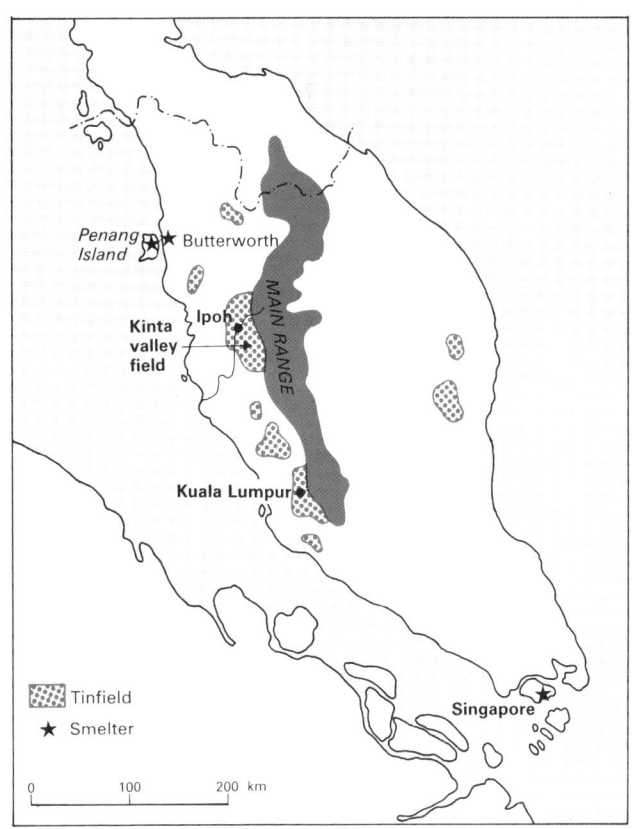

13 Tin mining

(16). The tin is dried, bagged and sent to smelters at Penang Island, Butterworth and Singapore (13).

TIN DREDGE DEMONSTRATION MODEL

You can make a model which shows how the tin dredge works. Ask for the details and model sheets.

14 Tin dredge

15 Using a monitor hose

16 Sluice boxes trap the tin particles

17 Tin production

Year	World	Malaysia
	thousand tonnes	
1971	225	75
1973	185	72
1975	205	64
1977	230	59
1979	247	63
1981	252	60
1983	173	42
1985	200	36

FOLLOW-UP WORK

1 How has tin mining affected:
   (a) the number and racial mixture of people in Malaysia;
   (b) roads and railways;
   (c) towns such as Kuala Lumpur and Ipoh?
2 Make the tin dredge model and use it to answer the following questions.
   (a) How does the dredge move across the swampland?
   (b) What are the main stages in obtaining tin from the swamps?
   (c) Why do you think only big companies use tin dredges?
   (d) Why is the land behind the dredge better for farming than the land ahead?
   (e) A tin dredge improves the land and a monitor hose destroys it. Do you agree with this statement? Give your reasons.
3 Malaysia is the largest producer of tin in the world. The largest markets are the United States, Japan, West Germany and Britain. Most tin is used in the canning and electrical industries. Study the statistics in table (17).
   (a) Suggest reasons why world demand for tin rises and falls.
   (b) What proportion of the world's tin was produced by Malaysia in 1971 and in 1985?
   (c) Suggest two reasons for falling production.
   (d) Why would Malaysia be wise not to depend on tin mining for her future development?

Rubber

Malaysia is the world's largest producer of natural rubber. This rubber comes from latex which is a white fluid in the cells of the inner bark of the rubber tree. A curved knife is used to remove a thin layer of bark (18). This is called tapping the tree. The cut is made at an angle halfway round the tree. This cuts across a large number of cells and the latex runs into a collecting cup. Tapping is done in the morning when it is not very hot and the latex flows freely from the trees.

Rubber trees grow wild in the Amazon forest (page 39). The 400 million trees now growing in Malaysia are descended from a few seeds taken from Brazil, germinated in Kew Gardens in London and taken to Malaya in 1877. Plantations of rubber trees were set up along the railways and roads in the south of the country (19). The hot, wet climate near the Equator suits the rubber tree. The land here is gently sloping (20) and the soils are well-drained. The first plantation was set up in 1895 and today over 60 per cent of the farm land is used for growing rubber. These developments took place as the car industry grew up in Europe and the United States. Most of the natural rubber needed to make tyres and many other products, comes from Malaysia.

More rubber trees are now grown on small family farms than on large estates. Most smallholdings are about two hectares. Each is run by a family with the husband, wife and children all helping to produce rubber. One-third of the land is used to grow vegetables and rear poultry.

18 Tapping a rubber tree

19 Rubber growing

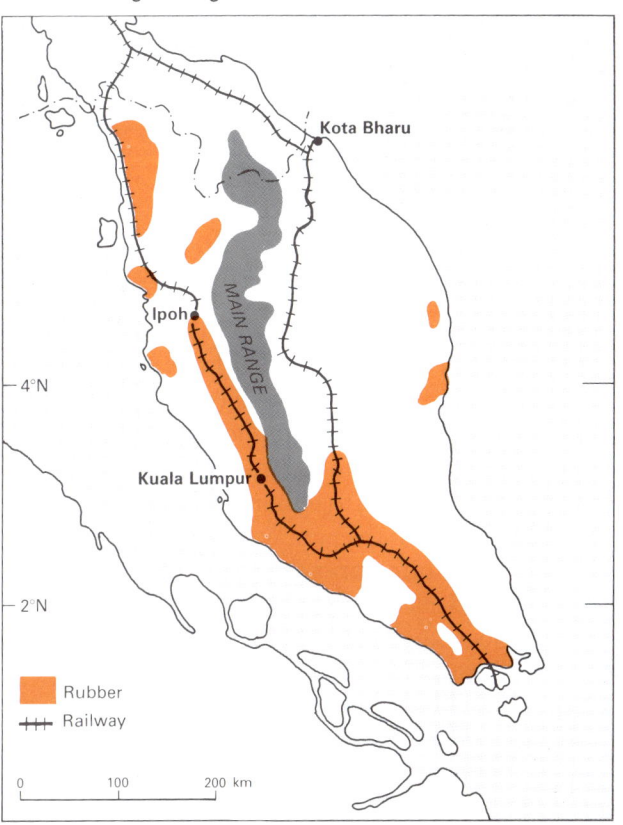

20 A rubber estate

21 A smallholder collecting latex from his rubber trees

22 Rolling a sheet of rubber at the processing centre

There are 200 rubber trees on the farm which are tapped early in the morning. The latex is collected in buckets (21) and taken by bicycle to the local processing centre. The latex is poured into pans and water and acid are added to it. This makes the rubber particles cling together to make a sheet. The sheet is taken from the pan, washed and rolled (22). The sheets are hung on a line to dry. The rubber is bought by a dealer and the farmer hopes he will get a good price. Sometimes the price is low and he has to borrow money to buy food for his family.

Photograph (23) shows part of a large rubber estate with 60 000 trees. There are many differences between this estate and a smallholding, as you can see from table (24).

23 *Part of a rubber estate*

24 *Smallholdings and estates compared*

Contrasts	Smallholdings	Estates
% of total land in Malaysia under rubber trees	72%	28%
% of total rubber production 1985	60%	40%
Size of holding	Average 2.6 hectares Largest 40 hectares	Average 1000 hectares Largest over 6000 hectares
Trees per hectare	160 Close together	60 Widely spaced rows
Output per tree	Low	High
Owners	The family	Big companies
Workers	The family. Malays on small farms. Chinese on larger farms	Hired labour. 50% Indians, 30% Chinese, 20% Malays
Tapping	When profitable to do so	At all times. Each tapper has 500 trees to tap each morning
Management	Poor. There are many old trees and a thick undergrowth	Good. Old trees are replaced by young trees from the nursery
Processing	Latex is coagulated, rolled into thin sheets and dried. Unsmoked	Scientific methods. High quality smoked rubber, crumb, crêpe and liquid latex
Quality	Varies. Often poor	Good
Marketing	Through dealers, millers and exporters	Direct by the company
Other crops	Rice, fruit trees, vegetables and coconut palms	Monoculture or duoculture with oil palms
Houses and services	Traditional home on the smallholding or kampong with its services	Concrete terraced houses, schools, hospital, mosque, community centre. Shops. Self-contained

FOLLOW-UP WORK

1 Study map (19) of the rubber-growing areas.
   (a) Why were rubber plantations set up alongside the railways?
   (b) Why is most rubber grown:
      (i) in the south of the peninsula;
      (ii) near the coast?
   (c) When plantations were set up on the best soils near the coast, what effect would this have on local rice farmers?

PLANTATION AGRICULTURE

A large estate is devoted to growing one cash crop. The system was invented by colonial powers to produce tropical and subtropical crops for the European market. It uses scientific methods and large inputs of capital and labour. Some processing of the product takes place on the estate.

Ask for the exercises.

---

25 World natural rubber production

	1985	1960
Total production million tonnes	4.0	2.0
Malaysia	36%	39%
Indonesia	28%	20%
Thailand	14%	12%
India	4%	1%
Sri Lanka	3%	5%
Others	15%	23%

26 Production of synthetic and natural rubber

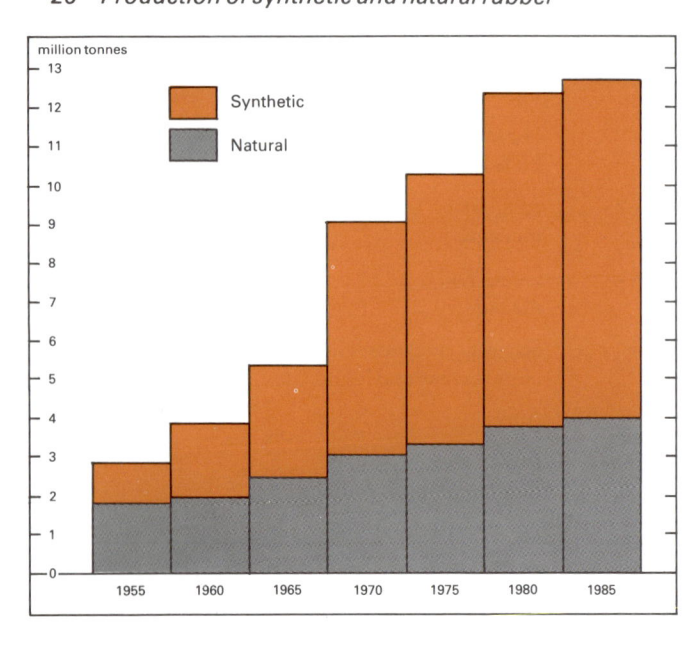

2 Study photographs (21) and (23) which show the rubber trees on a smallholding and on an estate.
   (a) What are the main differences you can see in the two scenes?
   (b) Draw sketches which are clearly labelled to show the differences you have mentioned.

3 Study table (24) which compares estates and smallholdings.
   (a) Estates cover only 28 per cent of the rubber-growing lands, grow fewer trees on each hectare than smallholdings but manage to produce 40 per cent of Malaysia's rubber. How can you explain this?
   (b) Why do smallholders grow other crops as well as rubber?

4 Study the statistics in table (25) which shows the main producers of natural rubber.
   (a) What change occurred in the total world production of natural rubber between 1960 and 1985?
   (b) What change occurred in Malaysia's production of natural rubber in this 25-year period?
   (c) Draw a graph to show the main producers of natural rubber in 1985.

5 In 1941, during the Second World War, Japan occupied the rubber-growing countries of southeast Asia. Supplies of rubber to the United States and Britain were cut off. By the end of the war America was making large amounts of synthetic rubber from petroleum. Graph (26) shows the production of synthetic rubber and natural rubber between 1955 and 1985.
   (a) Has the use of synthetic rubber caused a decline in the production of natural rubber? Say why.
   (b) Why is it easier to make more synthetic rubber than natural rubber?
   (c) Why is the future production of natural rubber more certain than for synthetic rubber?

A smallholder and his wife

Kuala Lumpur: mining camp to primate city

Kuala Lumpur is Malaysia's largest city, capital, major centre of business, industry, transport, communications, education and culture. With a population of more than one million in 1987 it was the primate city, three times the size of Ipoh, the second largest city.

The growth of KL, as the city is always called, has been rapid (27). It began in 1857 as a camp and trading centre hacked out of the rainforest by Chinese tin miners who had found large deposits of tin in the Kelang valley. The first boost to the growth of the settlement came when the British took over control from the Chinese in 1880. They laid out rubber plantations and built a railway to Port Kelang 42 kilometres west of KL. The town's location midway along the west coast mining and plantation belt (13, 19) made it an ideal centre for administration, commerce and industry. It became capital of the British-protected Federated Malay States in 1895 and has kept its status as capital city ever since that time.

27 The growth of Kuala Lumpur

Year	Population
1857	87
1887	4 000
1930	111 400
1947	175 900
1957	316 200
1970	451 700
1980	937 817
1987	1 200 000

28 Centre of the city

29 Malay buildings in KL

The population rose in the years after 1947 as thousands of people moved into the city for protection during a period of communist-led guerrilla warfare.

Since independence in 1957 the city has grown into a big, modern city. There is a central business district (28) with high-rise offices and flats, banks, hotels, restaurants and large shops. There is a string of new industrial developments along the railway and new motorway between the city and Port Kelang (31). Hundreds of thousands of people have moved into KL and along the corridor of growth to the port, attracted by the job opportunities there.

The Chinese dominate the city. They control commerce and industry and own shops. The Indians are still connected with the rubber estates and also find work in transport and the professions. The Malays, who have a firmer base in rural areas, have control of government administration and the police and have given their own people a bigger share of business and industry in recent years. The different ethnic groups live in their own neighbourhoods which often have a distinctive appearance (29).

FOLLOW-UP WORK

1 What stages can you recognise in the growth of the city? What caused them?
2 KL has a population of mixed races.
   (a) What are the main jobs done by each group? Suggest reasons for this.
   (b) Give some reasons why these groups often live in separate neighbourhoods.

New industries for Malaysia

Malaysia is blessed with a wide range of commodities. It leads the world in the production and export of natural rubber, palm oil and tin and is a big producer of tropical hardwoods, cocoa and pepper. There is a surplus of oil and gas to export. In the 1980s the world price for all these commodities fell. Fortunately the country had already begun to make products from these raw materials. Japan helped to build a steelworks at Prai. Map (30) shows the location of the works and nearby supplies of raw materials. This factory opened in 1967. It was the Mitsubishi company of Japan which built Malaysia's car factory near Kuala Lumpur in 1985. Thirty-six per cent of the parts are made in Malaysia and the rest come from Japan. The cars are sold in Malaysia. Many other manufacturing industries have been set up (31). The trade statistics (32) show that the country is now adding manufactures to the list of exports.

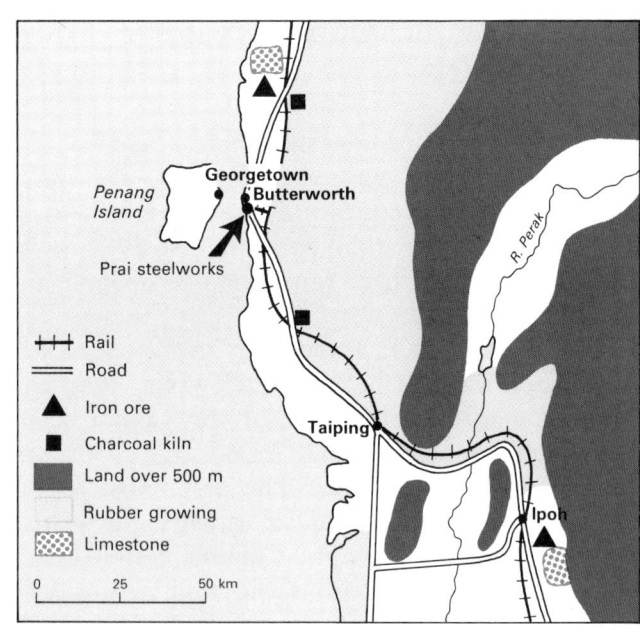

30 *Location of steelworks*

32 Imports and exports (percentage value, 1985)

Imports		Exports	
Machinery and transport equipment	44	Petroleum and products	32
Other manufactures	29	Machinery and transport equipment	18
Fuel and lubricants	10	Other manufactures	12
Food	10	Palm oil	12
Others	7	Logs and timber	10
		Rubber	9
		Tin	3
		Others	4
Main sources		*Main markets*	
Japan	23	Japan	25
Singapore	16	Singapore	19
USA	15	USA	13
Also UK	4	Also UK	3

FOLLOW-UP WORK

1 Copy map (30). Draw arrows on your map to show how charcoal made from old rubber trees, iron ore and limestone reach the steelworks. Write about the advantages of Prai as a location for a steelworks. Mention raw materials, water for cooling, transport, labour supply and markets.

2 Why does Malaysia want to reduce the amount of raw materials exported and increase the export of products made from those materials?

3 Imagine that you are a businessman with money to invest in Malaysia. The government has given you information about the factories they need (33) and where they can be built (34).
 (a) Choose **five** factories you would like to build.
 (b) Choose a location for **each** factory.
 Give reasons for your decisions.

4 Why does the government want factories in all parts of the country rather than in Kuala Lumpur, the largest city in Malaysia?

5 Suggest advantages and problems for having a car industry in Malaysia.

6 Suggest reasons why Malaysia has closer trade links with Japan than with the UK.

31 *Industry between Kuala Lumpur and Port Kelang*

Factories needed	Local materials	Markets	Number of workers	Incentives
1 Tyres 2 Footwear	Rubber	World	Moderate or small numbers	Factory building costs are low ** New factories do not pay tax for 2 years **
3 Soap 4 Margarine	Palm oil			
5 Desiccated coconut	Coconut			
6 Farm equipment	Steel	South-east Asia		
7 Plywood 8 Furniture 9 Prefabricated houses	Tropical hardwood	World	85% of the labour supply is in Peninsular Malaysia	Companies which employ over 350 people do not pay tax for 5 years **
10 Paper 11 Rayon	Mangrove wood			
12 Chemicals 13 Fertilisers	Oil Limestone	South-east Asia	15% of the labour supply is in Sabah and Sarawak	Companies which build factories in undeveloped areas in Sabah and Sarawak do not pay tax for 10 years **
14 Machinery 15 Cans 16 Vehicle parts	Steel Tin Rubber			
17 Paper filler 18 Pottery	China clay			Allowances are given to companies which: (i) use local materials (ii) export their products **
19 Bottles	Glass sands			
20 Synthetic textiles	Oil Wood	World		
21 Watches 22 Cameras 23 Calculators 24 Air conditioners 25 Refrigerators	Nil	World	Large numbers. There is a young, easily trained labour-force at low cost	Free Trade Zone. There are duty-free imports of raw materials and parts

33 Factories needed in Malaysia

34 Factory locations

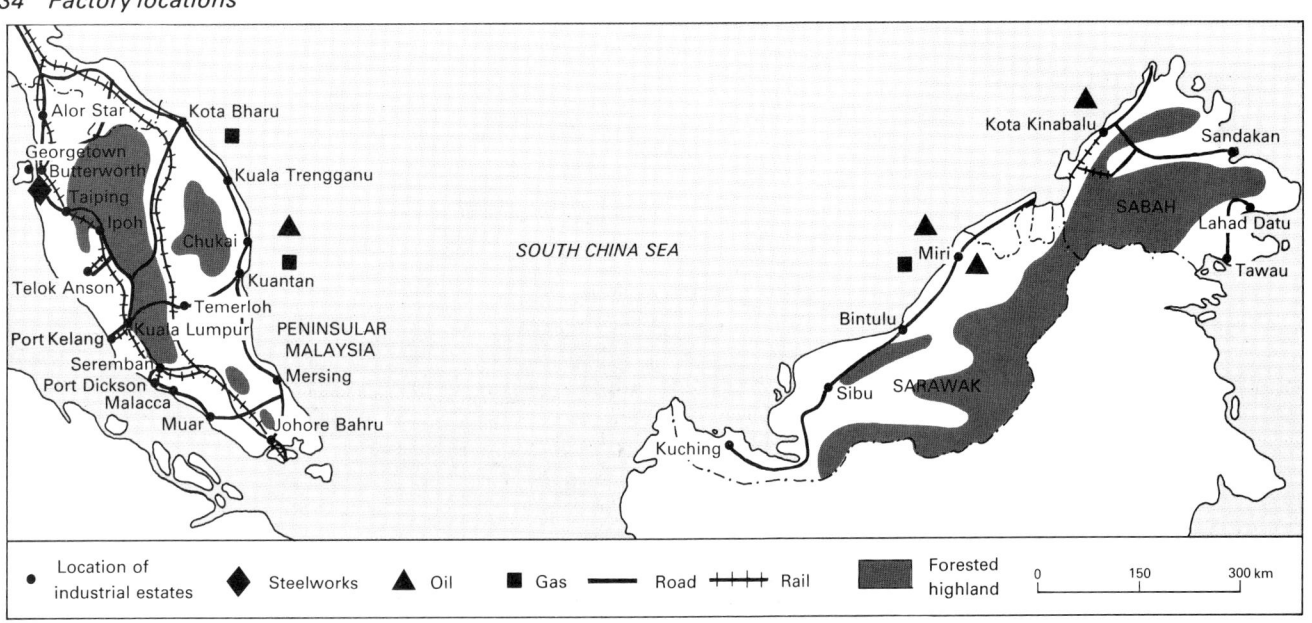

97

Nigeria

A new country with a long history

Nigeria, like all the countries of Africa, got its boundaries as a result of treaties drawn up after the Berlin Conference in 1884. It was agreed that countries which could occupy land in Africa were free to claim it as their own. British traders had established themselves in the delta area of the river Niger in the eighteenth century and, moving up river, gained a large hinterland.

> **HINTERLAND**
>
> A term first used to describe the land behind a port or seaboard to which it distributed imports and was supplied with exports. Now it is used to describe the area of influence around any town or city.

2 People, vegetation and farming

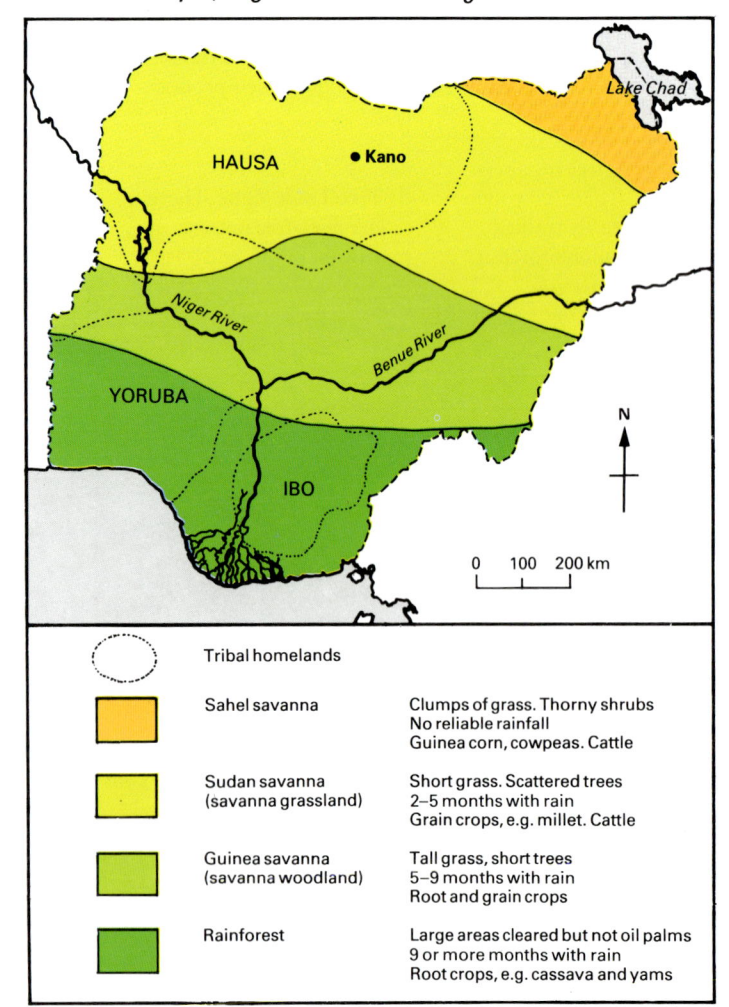

	Tribal homelands	
	Sahel savanna	Clumps of grass. Thorny shrubs No reliable rainfall Guinea corn, cowpeas. Cattle
	Sudan savanna (savanna grassland)	Short grass. Scattered trees 2–5 months with rain Grain crops, e.g. millet. Cattle
	Guinea savanna (savanna woodland)	Tall grass, short trees 5–9 months with rain Root and grain crops
	Rainforest	Large areas cleared but not oil palms 9 or more months with rain Root crops, e.g. cassava and yams

1 Forest in the south

By 1914 all the boundaries were drawn and a patchwork of colonies appeared on the Europeans' map of Africa. There were tiny countries stretching along rivers, landlocked countries, and large countries where much of the land was unseen by Europeans, who often drew boundaries as straight lines across the map. These decisions took no notice of the people who lived there. The eastern boundary of Nigeria, for example, cut across the land of 14 tribal groups. Inside these boundaries were three large ethnic groups and 200 smaller ones each with its own language, beliefs, customs and traditions. Covering an area four times the size of Britain, Nigeria stretches from the rainforests of the south (1) through savanna lands in the middle to semi-desert scrubland in the north (2). This new country was certainly a strange combination of people and places.

The Hausa live in the dry northern plains. They are settled cultivators and traders. They had organised states and built cities hundreds of years before Europeans arrived. Kano (3), for example,

3 Kano: old city in the north

4 Dye pits in Kano

was a manufacturing and trading centre at the southern end of Saharan trade routes to the Mediterranean coast. Dyed cloth (4) and leather are still made there. The Hausa are Muslims whose Islamic faith was originally brought to Africa by Arab traders. Early in the nineteenth century the nomadic Fulani tribe conquered the Hausa and spread their empire south to the Niger and its main tributary the Benue (2).

The Yoruba live in the south-west. They cultivate land in the forest and savanna. Many of them live in towns and cities which date back to the twelfth century. Power is held by local chiefs. The Yoruba are noted for their trade, business and colourful art and crafts (5).

The Ibo live in the forest areas of the south-east of Nigeria. It is densely settled land like Yorubaland but here there are scattered villages, each run by a council of elders. The Ibo are noted for their energy, community effort and democratic methods.

Bringing these people together in one country was to bring bitter conflict, civil war, uneasy co-operation and change. Colonial rule also brought a change in development. The people of Nigeria had for centuries developed their own ways of living. Their farming (2) was adapted to the environment and they could feed themselves. They would now develop along different lines.

FOLLOW-UP WORK

1 Locate Nigeria on a map of West Africa in an atlas.
   Name three countries to the north and west of Nigeria which are
   (a) larger than Nigeria and with some long straight-line boundaries;
   (b) small, long and narrow;
   (c) landlocked.
2 What advantages and problems might there be for Nigeria having
   (a) many ethnic groups;
   (b) many types of land?
3 Study map (2).
   (a) How can you explain the change in vegetation that occurs from south to north in Nigeria?
   (b) How does this also help to explain the changes in the type of crops that are grown?
   (c) Which ethnic group lives in an area
      (i) where cattle are reared;
      (ii) mostly forested;
      (iii) with a coastline;
      (iv) affected by drought (6)?
4 What evidence have you read to suggest that there was development before the Europeans drew the boundaries of Nigeria?

6 A year of drought

5 Selling cloth at a Yoruba market

A change in development: railways

The first use that Britain had for what was later to become Nigeria was as a source of slaves. Ten million people were taken out of Africa to work on plantations in the American colonies. Britain was most active in this trade in the eighteenth century. Liverpool and Bristol became rich cities operating a system which sustained the industrial revolution. Ironware, cloth and guns were exported to Africa in exchange for slaves to work on plantations in the Caribbean and North America which provided cotton, sugar and tobacco for Britain. The centre of Nigeria became empty of people because of this trade. Iboland and Yorubaland lost huge numbers of young men and women.

Oil palms which grow naturally across the southern forest zone became a more profitable and acceptable form of trade in the nineteenth century. Britain wanted the palm oil for lighting, soap and as a lubricant in her new factories.

The river Niger and its main tributary the Benue provided routes to the interior. At the turn of the century railways extended the hinterland. Railways gave Britain control over the land and people. Cash crops could be grown and minerals extracted along the line of rail. Groundnuts (peanuts) and cotton grew well in the drier north and cocoa and rubber in the wet south. Soon there was the unusual sight of pyramids of peanuts (7) alongside the railway track at Kano and sheets of rubber hanging out to

7 Pyramids of peanuts

8 Sheets of rubber hanging out to dry

dry in the villages of Yorubaland (8), ready for transport to the port. The flow of raw materials to Britain became the new system for development in Nigeria. People soon became part of the money economy growing cash crops and working at the mines. They could pay taxes and buy the products of Britain's factories.

Building the railway network

Railways were built to serve the main cash crop areas, the main centres of population and to develop the mines (9).

Copy map (10). Mark onto the map each length of railway in the order in which they were built using the information in table (9). Building started in Lagos in 1896.

9 Nigerian railways

Railway line built from	to	Date completed
Lagos	Ibadan	1901
Ibadan	Jebba	1909
Baro	Minna	1910
Minna	Kaduna and Kano	1911
Jebba	Minna	1912
Zaria	Jos	1914
Port Harcourt	Enugu	1916
Enugu	Makurdi	1921
Makurdi	Kafanchan and Kaduna	1927
Kafanchan	Jos	1927
Zaria	Kaura Namoda	1929
Kano	Nguru	1930

NETWORK AND NODES

A network is a pattern of interconnected lines. A meeting point of lines, such as at a town, is called a node. A developed network has a large number of interconnections and nodes allowing goods and people to move easily between places.

FOLLOW-UP WORK

1. (a) Why did routes start at the coast?
   (b) Which ports grew as a result of the railway?
2. Suggest three reasons why the railway was built the full length of the country from south to north.
3. Suggest why track was laid at different points along the same route, from Baro and Lagos on the line to Kano, for example.
4. In what year could you first travel by rail direct from Lagos to Kano?
5. Suggest why railways were built between
   (a) Port Harcourt and Enugu;
   (b) Zaria and Kaura Namoda;
   (c) Zaria and Jos. Suggest why this line later closed down.
6. Name the cash crops which might be carried on a train from Kano to Lagos.
7. Which port would be handling most tin ore exports in (a) 1925 (b) 1935? Say why.
8. Railway bridges replaced rail ferries in 1916 and 1934. At which town and in which year was each bridge opened?
9. Was Nigeria's railway system a developed network in 1930? Explain your answer.
10. Why was a complementary system of roads, linked to the railway, also built?

A CONCEPTUAL MODEL

There are many three-dimensional models which you can make in this book. A conceptual model is different. It is identifying and linking together the main aspects of something which you want to understand such as the growth of a transport network in a colonial country.

11. Diagram (11) shows a four-stage model for the development of a transport network in a colonial country. What do you think the next stage will be?

Ask for the exercise sheet on the railways of West Africa.

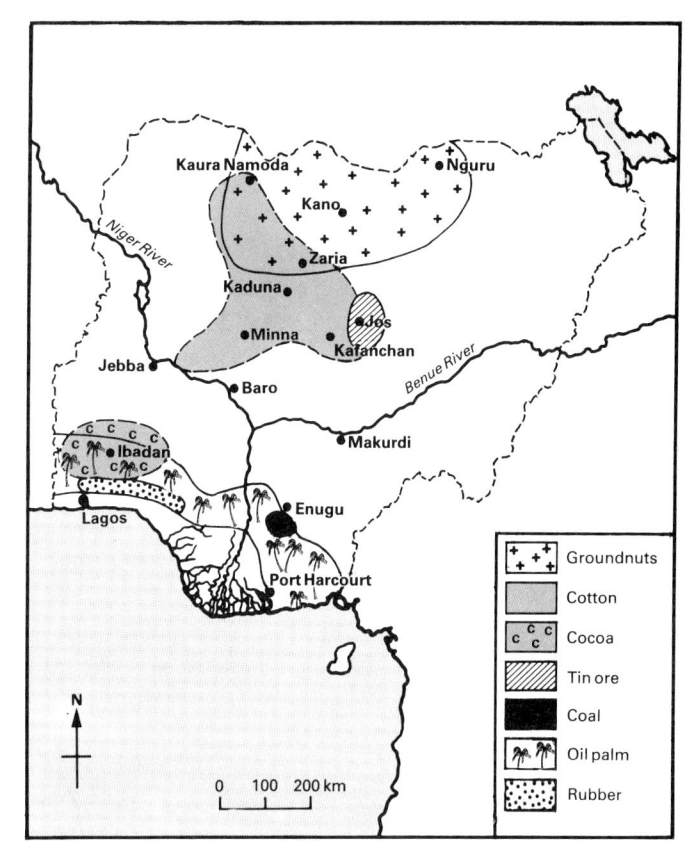

10 Export crops and minerals

11 Four-stage model of a transport network

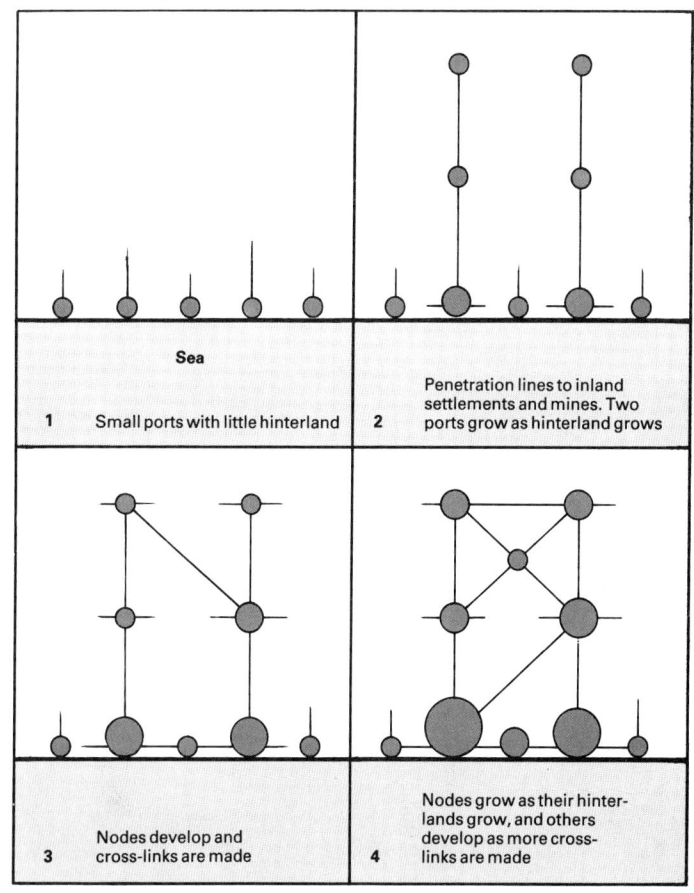

1. Small ports with little hinterland
2. Penetration lines to inland settlements and mines. Two ports grow as hinterland grows
3. Nodes develop and cross-links are made
4. Nodes grow as their hinterlands grow, and others develop as more cross-links are made

Oil: benefits and problems

In 1960 Nigeria became an independent country but the pattern of development based upon the export of her resources to Europe still continues. Multinational companies such as Unilever, the joint British and Dutch food and detergent giant, continue to operate cash crop farming for export markets. But Nigeria has changed rapidly in recent years following the discovery of oil in the Niger delta in 1956 (12). International oil companies, the largest of which is Shell-BP, brought high technology into use to get the oil out of the reservoir rocks beneath the delta swamps and shallow offshore waters. Forests were bulldozed (13) and swamp barges brought into use (14). Channels are dredged and the barges floated to the drilling site. The barge is filled with water and it settles into position. When the drilling is completed the barge is emptied of water and floated to a new drill site.

Drilling on firmer ground is a cheap and easy operation (15) although the heat and humidity, snakes and mosquitoes make life unpleasant. There

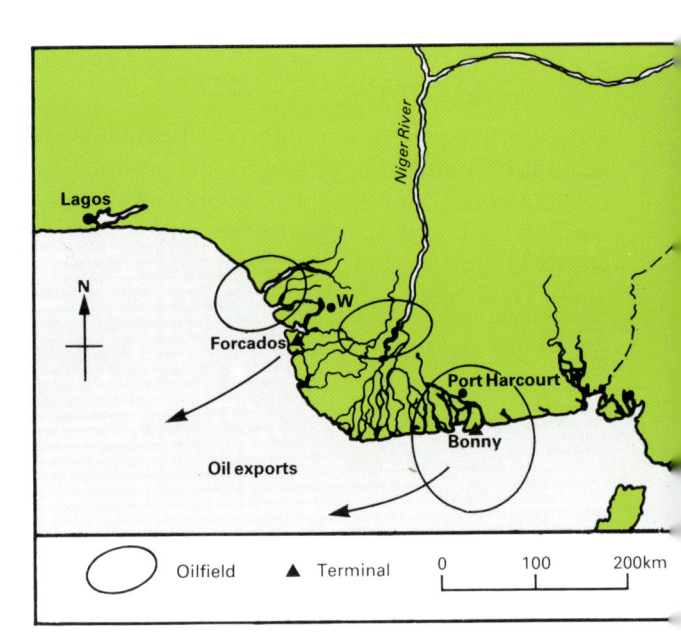

12 Oilfields in the delta area

13 Bulldozing the forest

14 Drilling for oil in the swamps

15 Drilling on firm ground

102

16 Helicopters move men and equipment

17 Oil terminal at Bonny

were no problems laying pipeline through the forest except perhaps bribing the local chief to gain his co-operation. Helicopters are always on hand to move workers from the drill sites to the terminals (16).

The oil began to flow in 1958. It is high-quality, light, sulphur-free oil which is in big demand for petrochemical industries in Europe and the USA.

The oil flows to the coastal terminals where it is stored before being piped out across the shallow waters to waiting tankers (17). The flow of oil rose to 1 million tonnes in 1960, to 20 million tonnes in 1966 and to 50 million tonnes in 1970.

In the 1970s the price of oil jumped as oil-producing countries decided to end the era of cheap oil. Profits from oil rocketed and Nigeria stepped up production (18). Within ten years Nigeria had become a rich country. How that money is spent and how long oil reserves will last determines whether all Nigerians share the benefits of this new-found wealth.

FOLLOW-UP WORK

1 (a) Make a list of the problems of oil production in the delta area.
   (b) Explain how each of these problems has been tackled.

RESOURCES

Those things which are available in the world for people to use for their food, clothing, housing and transport, for example.

Renewable resources such as crops and trees can be produced and used time and time again.

Non-renewable (or finite) resources such as petroleum, once used cannot be replaced.

---

2 Explain the importance of multinational companies in the development of Nigeria's oil resources.
3 Describe some of the features of the site and location of the Bonny oil terminal as shown in photograph (17) and map (12).
4 Study the statistics in table (18).

18 Oil production and revenues (1970–80)

Year	Production million tonnes	Revenue million naira*
1970	50	166
1971	75	510
1972	89	764
1973	100	1 000
1974	112	3 726
1975	89	4 271
1976	103	5 365
1977	104	6 080
1978	94	4 654
1979	114	8 880
1980	102	10 200

(*7 naira = £1)

(a) By how many times had the money raised by selling the same amount of oil increased between 1973 and 1980?
(b) Why might this trend encourage Nigeria either to produce more oil or conserve her resources? What would you advise?
(c) How would this money help Nigeria become a more developed country?
5 Nigeria had used one-third of her oil resources by the mid-1980s. What will be the main advantage and the main problem of reducing oil exports?

THE WORLD OIL TRADE

Oil is the main cargo in international trade. Who has the oil and who wants it? Ask for the exercise sheet.

Using the oil wealth

New houses, cars and television sets are some of the signs of prosperity for many people in towns and cities in Nigeria (19). The wealth is from oil. There are thousands of jobs at the drill sites and terminals and thousands more in industries, transport and offices which service the oil business. Profits from the sale of oil are spread out from central government to the 19 states of Nigeria.

In the towns and cities there are new schools for most young children (20), clinics and hospitals. There are higher wages for public servants. The money passes through many hands providing more jobs in personal services, shops, business and banking, for example.

Young people have moved into towns hoping to share in the opportunities, leaving the older members of the family in the countryside. If one person finds a job in the town, the rest of the family will follow. Much of the food that is needed in the growing urban areas has come from abroad with imported wheat for breadmaking, and rice and tinned food replacing more traditional foods. Consumer goods, from clothes and radios to Mercedes cars, are in big demand. These are all imported along with raw materials and manufactured goods such as cement and steel for building and industry.

The attitude of spending all today for fear that the money may not be there tomorrow leads to waste. Corruption is widespread and millions of naira disappear into private banks overseas. At the same time the schools lack books and equipment and children carrying their own desks to school is a common sight. There are hospitals and clinics but often no drugs to use in them. Little of the wealth has reached the countryside and this is where most people live.

The contrasts between rich and poor, town and countryside have become more marked in recent years.

Look at the statistics in table (21) to see what progress was made in the first 20 years when the wealth from oil was reaching a peak.

19 *Signs of prosperity*

20 *Most children attend primary school*

21 *Social changes (1960–80)*

Changes	1960	1980
Number of people (millions)	42m	84m
Urban population (% of total)	13%	20%
Number of cities over ½ million	2	9
Birth rate per 1000 people	52	50
Death rate per 1000 people	25	17
Life expectancy in years	39	49
Infant mortality (deaths per 1000 under 1 year)	152	120
Child death rate (1–4 years)	36	22
People per doctor	74 000	16 000
Children at primary school	36%	62%
Children at secondary school	4%	13%
Adult literacy (can read and write)	15%	34%
GNP per capita (US $)	75	895

FOLLOW-UP WORK

1 How might an increase in the wealth of a country bring about fewer deaths, longer lifespans and better education?
2 What percentage of young people do not go to secondary school? Why is this a problem for the future development of Nigeria?
3 What changes, mentioned in the text, have happened in rural areas as a result of the growth of oil wealth?

GROSS NATIONAL PRODUCT (GNP)

This is the total amount of money a country earns (income) in one year. It comes from the sale of goods and services in the three sectors: agriculture, industry and services. GNP does not show how many people were needed to produce this amount or it had to support.

GNP per capita (person) is the GNP divided by the number of people in the country. This gives a general idea of how rich or poor a country is. It appears to show the wealth each person has, but wealth is not evenly distributed and people scratching a living in rural areas and in city shanty towns do not enter into GNP calculations.

4 (a) How much did the population increase between 1960 and 1980?
  (b) How might this increase affect the country's ability to improve living standards?
5 Does increased wealth appear to have caused any improvements in people's lives as shown in the statistics (21)?
6 Why are figures for infant mortality and the adult literacy rate (the percentage of adults who can read and write) a better measure of a country's development (see page 5) than GNP per capita?

Scatter graphs can be used to investigate wealth and development. Ask for the exercise sheet.

Big projects

The government is spending large amounts of money gained from the sale of oil on big development projects. Study the details of the projects lettered from A to K below. Rank the projects in order of importance. Give reasons for the order you choose.

A Irrigation project
Location: Bakolori.
Advantages: Reservoir stores wet-season water to irrigate 30 000 hectares in the dry season (22). Wheat and rice can be sold in Lagos and other cities.
Problems: The reservoir covers more land than it irrigates. Farmers below the dam no longer get floodwaters for their rice crops.
Cost. US$ 1 billion

B Cement works
Location: Near Lagos, Sokoto and Nkalagu.
Advantages: Uses local limestone. Big demand from other projects. Stops the need for imports.
Problems: Quarries spoil the landscape and the factory pollutes the air (23).
Cost. US$ 1 billion

22 Irrigation in the dry north

23 Cement works

24 Projects location map

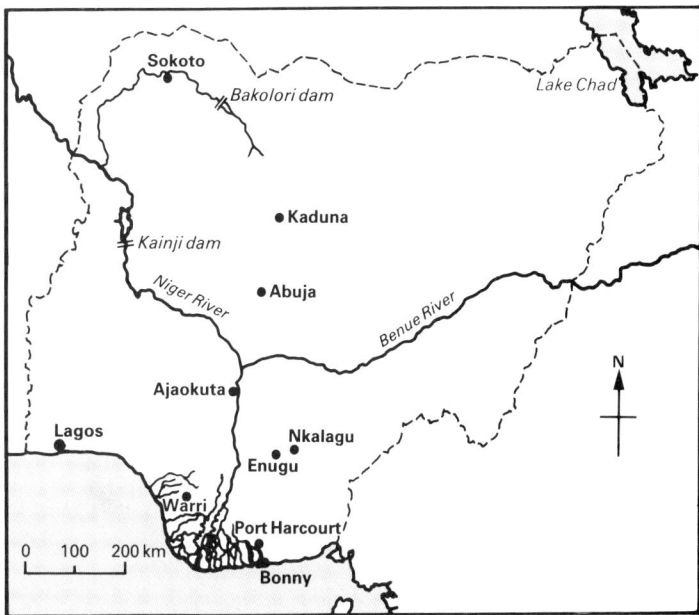

105

25 Using a feeder road

C Agricultural development project
Location: All states. Farm centres 20 kilometres apart.
Advantages: Farm centres provide small farmer with low-interest loans, cheap fertiliser, insecticide, seed and equipment. A tube well and pump to irrigate 1 hectare using groundwater. Feeder roads make the centre accessible (25). Storage and marketing by the centre. It raises food output.
Problems: Better-off farmers benefit most and poor farmers get poorer.
Cost. US$ 5 billion

26 New road between cities

D Road network
Location: Road links between all big towns and cities (26) including a trunk road between Lagos and Port Harcourt.
Advantages: 6000 km of new roads will help the movement of people, food and materials between towns and cities.
Problems: There will be some duplication of work undertaken by the states. Railways will decline.
Cost. US$ 5 billion

E Oil refineries
Location: Warri, Port Harcourt and Kaduna.
Advantages: Using own oil resources to make petrol and chemicals. This will support new industries such as plastics and synthetic rubber. Stops dependence on imports.
Problems: Danger of chemical leaks and pollution. Imports might be cheaper.
Cost. US$ 3 billion

F Liquefied gas plant
Location: Bonny.
Advantages: Uses huge local gas resources. When cooled to liquid it can be exported to markets in Europe and the USA. Supplies will last longer than oil.
Problems: Declining European market due to increased use of North Sea oil and gas. Surplus world supplies.
Cost. US$ 14 billion

G Fertiliser factory
Location: Near Port Harcourt.
Advantages: Uses local natural gas supplies and will produce 600 000 tonnes of fertiliser each year. This will raise crop yields and stop the country's dependence on imports.
Problems: Danger of leaks of poison gas. Forest clearance for the factory site.
Cost. US$ 1 billion

H New capital city
Location: Abuja.
Advantages: This will be a growth pole (see page 36) in the centre of the country relieving over-concentration of business and administration in Lagos. The city has been planned like Milton Keynes in Britain (27) with wide roads, offices, residential areas for 3 million people and government buildings.
Problems: Difficult to plan the building projects. Loss of money due to corruption. High cost on a greenfield site needing all new roads, water supply and power, for example.
Cost. US$ 10 billion (each year)

27 Planned like Milton Keynes

28 The construction of Kainji dam

I Hydro-electric power project
Location: Kainji on the Niger (28).
Advantages: A dam across the Niger will provide electricity for west Nigeria from Lagos to Kaduna. This will be a multi-purpose scheme including irrigation, transport, fishing and tourist use.
Problems: It disturbs the use of the floodplain below the dam which is the best farmland. The 1200 km² lake requires 42 000 people to be moved from their farms and villages to higher, less fertile land.
Cost. US$ 1 billion

J Steelworks
Location: Ajaokuta.
Advantages: The steelworks will use newly discovered but low-grade iron ore supplies. There is coal nearby at Enugu. The steel rods and rolled steel will be the basis for other industries. Stops the need for imports.
Problems: Help is being provided by the USSR but it is old technology which will result in high-cost production. It would be much cheaper to import steel from Taiwan and Japan at present.
Cost. US$ 8 billion

29 Hardwoods for Europe

K Timber pulp and paper mill
Location: Near Lagos.
Advantages: It uses local forest resources (29). There is a big demand for hardwoods in Europe, Japan and the USA. Home demand comes from schools, business and administration.
Problems: Deforestation. The forest will be lost at a faster rate than it can be replaced.
Cost. US$ 1 billion

FOLLOW-UP WORK

1. What link is there between these projects:
   (a) G, D and C;
   (b) B, D and H;
   (c) I, K and H;
   (d) E, D and A?
2. Why will Nigeria benefit from developments in
   (a) farming;
   (b) industry;
   (c) transport?
3. Why are projects B, E, G and J called import substitution industries?
4. In what ways is project C a better development project for Nigeria than project A?
5. (a) Name the new cities in Britain and in Brazil which influenced the building of Nigeria's new capital city Abuja.
   (b) Why will the new capital be a good development for (i) Lagos; (ii) the central region of Nigeria; (iii) national unity of Nigeria's three main races?
6. **Crisis**
   In the 1980s, world demand for oil slumped during a period of world economic recession.
   Prices fell because there was too much oil on the market including North Sea oil.
   Nigeria had begun all of these projects expecting oil sales and profits to keep rising. By 1985 Nigeria had borrowed US$11 billion on the strength of this and had to spend 70 per cent of the profits from the sale of oil to reduce this debt. Some projects had to be postponed or cancelled to save US$ 25 billion.
   Which projects would you choose in order to save this amount? Give your reasons.

DROUGHT

Continuous dry weather. Distress is caused when drought occurs in areas which normally have adequate rainfall.

Ask for the exercise sheet about the drought in the Sahel.

Towns and cities: Lagos

Nigeria has the largest population in Africa with more than 100 million people out of a total of 600 million in the continent. One-quarter of all Nigerians live in urban areas. The cluster of towns in south-west Nigeria stands out on the map (30). These are Yoruba towns which date back centuries. Many people who live there farm the surrounding countryside. This southern part of West Africa is well settled because the warmth and plentiful rainfall favour farming with high-yielding root crops. There is also a line of inland towns including those in northern Nigeria. These are long-established towns which grew up as trans-Saharan trading centres. This northern area is also favourable for settlement with grain crops and cattle rearing.

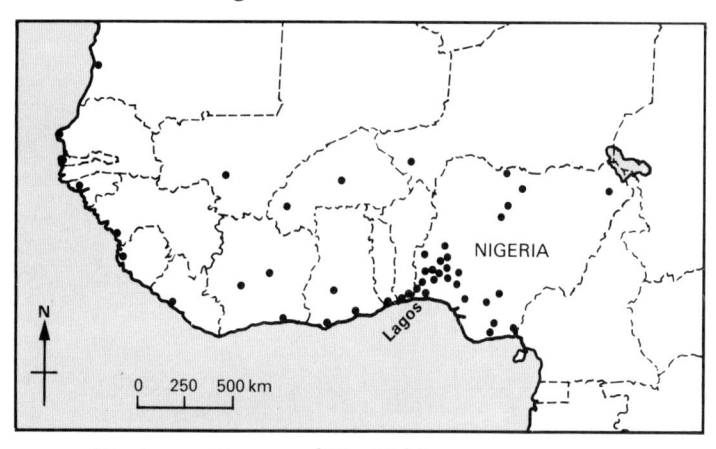

30 Largest towns of West Africa

Many of the largest settlements are on the coast. They have grown most because of colonial influences and the importance of trade. Lagos is the biggest city. It has grown rapidly since 1950 (31).

Small Yoruba settlements were built on islands which are part of a bar of shifting sand enclosing the Lagos lagoon. These were sites that could be easily defended against attack from land and sea. Shallow offshore water, shifting river courses, marsh and forest would be little problem to an early farming and fishing community. The growth of Lagos as a centre of the slave trade, colonial capital, major port and eventually an industrial, commercial and business city with millions of residents on this same site (32) has, however, caused major problems.

31 Population of Greater Lagos (thousands)

1850	20	1970	1600
1950	250	1980	3000
1960	600	1987	4000

32 Aerial view of Lagos

33 Contrasts in housing

District	People per hectare	House type	Piped water and sewage
Ikeja	200	Bungalows	100%
Surulere	500	Houses	50%
Ebute Metta	750	Rented rooms	30%
Lagos Island	1000	Rented rooms	70%
Ikoyi	200	Houses and flats	100%

34 Land use in Lagos

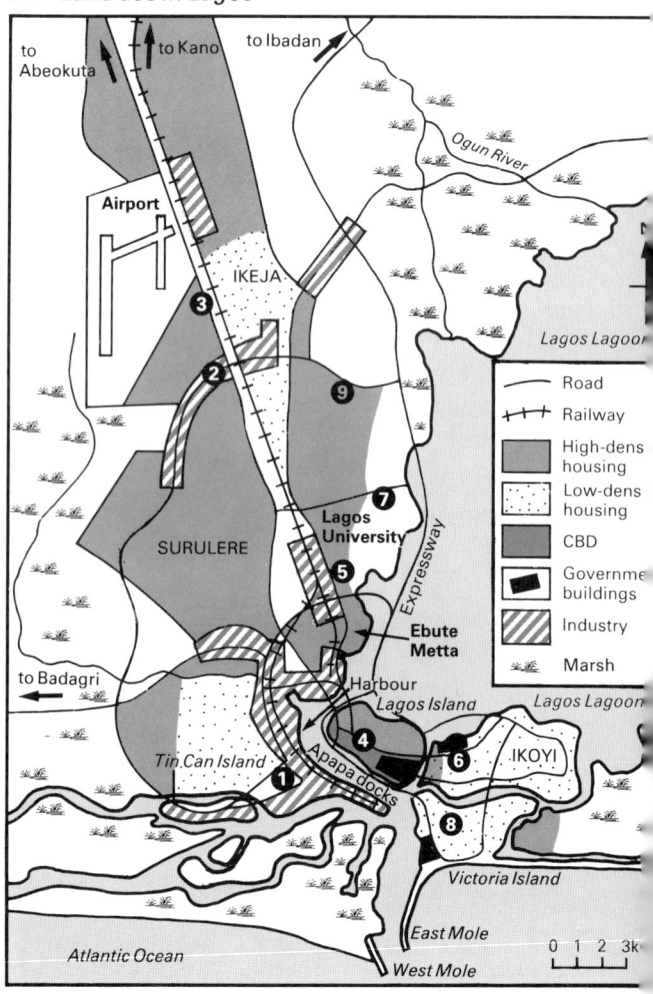

FOLLOW-UP WORK

Study the photograph (32) and map (34) as you read about the main functions of the city. Answer the questions which arise from each area of study.

Housing
Lagos has grown rapidly since 1950 because of oil wealth and the developments this has brought. Young people have moved there to find jobs. There are planned housing areas with 3- or 4-storey blocks of flats but one-third of the population live in slum housing. The figures (33) show some contrasts in housing.
(a) In which direction has the city grown? Say why.
(b) Why has Lagos got a long and narrow shape?
(c) In which two areas (33) are people with high incomes likely to live?
(d) Which of these two areas is in the best location for people who work in government offices?
(e) Lack of sewers and water brought by tanker lorry could lead to illness in Lagos which is only 6° north of the Equator. Say why.

Port
An offshore bar extends along the coast of West Africa from Ghana to the Niger delta. The sand of the bar comes from waves breaking on the gently sloping beach offshore plus sand moving along the shore (longshore drift). The bar is broken only in a few places which allows vessels to reach the mainland. One such place is Lagos. Dredging provides an 8-metre-deep channel.
(a) The moles (stone piers) were built in 1917. Why do you think they were needed?
(b) What evidence is there on the map that there is longshore drift from west to east along this coast?
(c) Why would the building of the railway to Kano (1912) help the port to grow?
(d) The main port area is Apapa. More docks were built in the late 1970s at Tin Can Island. Why do you think they were needed?
(e) Nigeria's largest trading partner is the UK. Suggest reasons why.

Industry
Lagos is the largest industrial city in Nigeria. These are some of the industries:
A Breweries/Soft drinks/Food processing
B Steel fabrications/Car assembly
C Hardwood furniture/Petroleum products
(a) Which groups of industries A, B or C depend most on (i) imported materials (ii) sales in the city (iii) Nigerian raw materials?
(b) Why do the factory areas benefit from being close to main arteries of transport?

(c) Which form of transport are there at these industrial sites:
(i) Ikeja (ii) Ebute Metta (iii) Apapa?

Offices
The main area of offices, banks and shops is called the Central Business District (CBD). It is on Lagos Island. In most cities the CBD has a central location which is easily reached from all parts of the city. Competition for space usually results in skyscraper buildings. High land values usually means that old houses are knocked down and replaced with more offices and big stores.

What evidence is there on the map (34) or photograph (32) to suggest that the usual features of a CBD occur in Lagos? Suggest reasons for any differences you notice.

Transport
The site and size of Lagos and the distribution of activities in the city produce major transport problems.
(a) Mark onto your own copy of map (34) the route by road taken by
 (i) a lorry from Apapa docks (1) to Ilupeju industrial estate (2)
 (ii) a worker going by car from Ikeja (3) to an office in the CBD (4)
 (iii) a government worker going from Yaba (5) to a government office (6)
 (iv) a student going to Lagos University (7) from Victoria Island (8)
 (v) a shop assistant going from Shomolu (9) by bus to the CBD (4).
(b) Using your map and photograph (35), say why there is traffic congestion in the city.
(c) How might these suggestions help to solve the problem:
 (i) a new expressway across Lagos lagoon;
 (ii) restricting cars according to number plates to entering the CBD on alternate days;
 (iii) a better bus service;
 (iv) an underground railway;
 (v) ferries;
 (vi) new capital city at Abuja?
Discuss the advantages and problems of each idea.

35 Traffic congestion

Nepal

Country of extremes

Nepal is a landlocked country, the size of England, lying on the southern slopes of the Himalayas between India and China (1) (see also map (1) page 67). Within the 200-kilometre width of the country the land rises from only 70 metres above sea level to the world's highest peak, Mt Everest, at 8848 metres (2). People live in three main regions which lie east to west across the country. The Terai is a lowland which is part of the river Ganges plain (3). Lying 26° north of the Equator the climate is subtropical with a forest which has been cleared for farming. Steep forested slopes separate the Terai from the hill and valley region lying between 900 metres and 2500 metres above sea level. Kathmandu, the capital of Nepal, occupies the largest and most fertile valley (4). The climate is temperate with woodlands of oak and alder. Rising above the hills are the steep mountain slopes of the Himalayas (5). The climate is alpine with conifer trees giving way to grassland. Above 5000 metres is the rock, snow and arctic climate of the upper mountain slopes (2) which are a scenic attraction for tourists and a challenge for mountaineers.

The great contrasts in the physical landscape are matched by an equal diversity of Nepalese people.

3 The Terai

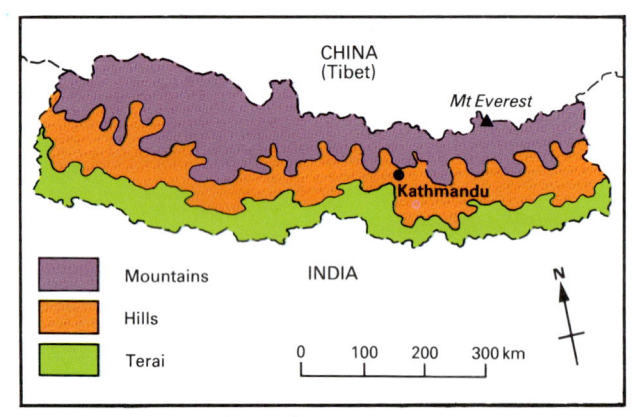

1 Three regions of Nepal

2 A view of Mt Everest

4 Kathmandu valley

5 In the mountains

There are twenty-five ethnic groups each with their own language, culture, religion and way of life which is often closely adapted to the place where they live (6). The Tharus of the Terai, for example, have a language similar to Hindi in India where they came from. Their religion is animist which means they believe every mountain, tree and stone has a spirit that must be honoured. They are rice farmers of the plain. Their houses have just one storey and are made from mud and thatch (6).

The Newars are the indigenous people of the Kathmandu valley. They speak Newari which is a Tibeto-Burman language. They were originally Buddhist but have since adopted elements of Hinduism. They are both farmers and townspeople. Their houses are made from brick and stone, tile and slate with carved wood.

The Sherpas live in the mountains of north-east Nepal. They originated in Tibet and they have a Tibetan language and Buddhist religion. They are farmers growing potatoes and barley and rearing yaks. They also lead trekking and mountaineering expeditions.

Study table (7) and photographs (8) and (9) which show many contrasts between the regions of Nepal. Answer the questions which follow.

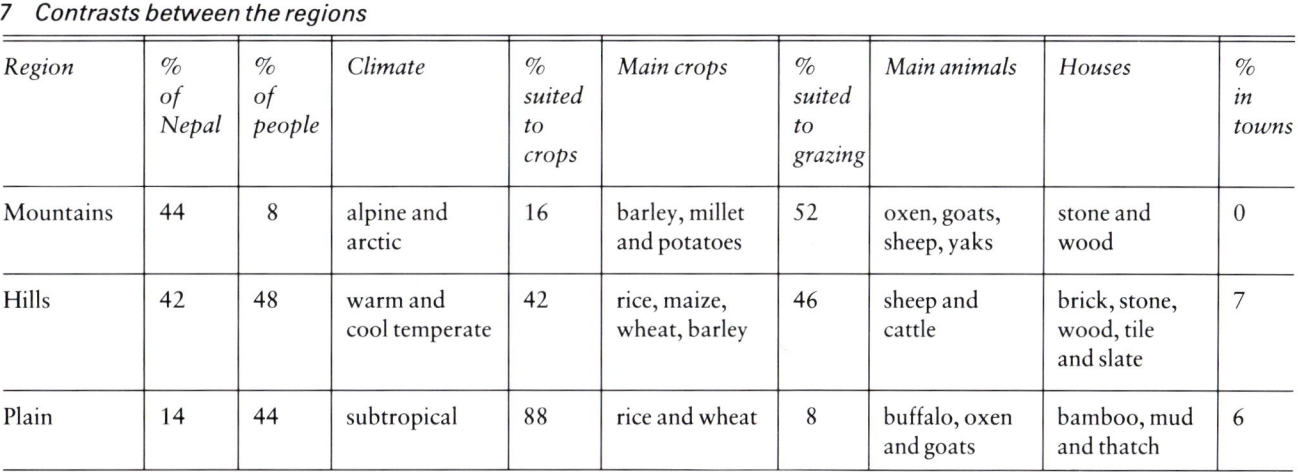

8 Houses in the mountains

9 Houses in the hill town

6 House in the Terai

FOLLOW-UP WORK

1. Compare the physical landscape and use of the land in the Terai as shown in photograph (3) with that of the mountains in photograph (5).
2. What links can you see between the land, climate and crop growing in the Terai?
3. Suggest reasons why the mountain region, which accounts for almost half of the land area of Nepal, has only 8 per cent of the population.
4. What physical and human evidence is there to suggest that the hill region is an area of transition between the mountains and the plain?

7 Contrasts between the regions

Region	% of Nepal	% of people	Climate	% suited to crops	Main crops	% suited to grazing	Main animals	Houses	% in towns
Mountains	44	8	alpine and arctic	16	barley, millet and potatoes	52	oxen, goats, sheep, yaks	stone and wood	0
Hills	42	48	warm and cool temperate	42	rice, maize, wheat, barley	46	sheep and cattle	brick, stone, wood, tile and slate	7
Plain	14	44	subtropical	88	rice and wheat	8	buffalo, oxen and goats	bamboo, mud and thatch	6

A country ready for change

Nepal was closed to the outside world from 1816 until 1951. This followed a two-year war with the British which fixed Nepal's border with India. Nepal was ruled by an army general and his offspring until the monarchy was restored in 1951. The country was then open to visitors and outside influences.

Any changes could only be for the better for most people. Life expectancy was only 25 years, and half of all children died before they were five years old. All the land was owned by 450 families who often demanded half to three-quarters of the tenant farmers' crops as rent. With little food and no clean water, malnutrition and disease took a heavy toll of life. The Terai was infested with mosquitoes which inflicted malaria on anyone living there. There was no formal education and most people could not read or write.

There have been many changes since 1951. Land reform is one of them. The land was taken from the few landowners and redistributed to the farmers which has meant most people have much more food to eat. Another change has been the introduction of the panchayat system which gives everyone a say in how the country is run. There are village and town panchayats or councils, each of which sends members to a district panchayat which in turn sends members to the national panchayat. Regardless of these changes, visitors to Nepal today might still think they have been transported back in time to a medieval age.

Ninety-three per cent of the population are in farming families. Methods are traditional with animal power and human labour put to use on small plots of land which total only two hectares (10). This provides a bare level of subsistence.

Life is very hard for women. They work in the fields using hoes and harvesting by hand. They carry heavy loads of feed for the animals (11). They spend long hours fetching water and firewood and their journeys are often up and down steep slopes. They pound the grain (12) and prepare meals over an open fire. They spin wool and make clothes for the family (13).

Some women may earn a few rupees breaking up boulders from the river-bed into small stones for roads and buildings (14). They may also do the building (15). On top of all this work the women raise a large family of children (16).

10 Farming in the Kathmandu valley

11 Women carry heavy loads

12 Pounding the grain

13 Spinning wool on the doorstep

15 Women and children often do the building

14 Women breaking up rocks

16 Large family in a small house

Life is hard for the children too. Most of them enrol at primary school but that school might be a two- or three-hour walk along a steep mountain track. It is not surprising that attendance is low and more children will be working in the fields than learning to read and write (17).

Illness is a constant companion. Chest infections and diarrhoea are particularly widespread. Dirty water is the main problem. Even mountain streams are contaminated by dung, dead animals and human waste. The toilet may be a hole in the ground or a designated area along a hedge. Drinking water can easily become contaminated from this source.

There are few doctors and no dentists so people have to suffer their illnesses, rotting teeth and mouth abscesses. Even with these many hardships the children are usually happy, smiling and friendly. They play the usual games such as hopscotch, stones and marbles but they rarely have pens and pencils to use. They soon grow up and look after their rapidly ageing parents. Girls marry at about 15 and are soon looking after a family of their own.

Religion provides a framework and meaning for

17 Children may have walked for two hours to reach this school

life. In the Hindu religion, for example, everyone is locked into the caste system (see page 72). People in low castes accept the hardships of life in the knowledge that they will be born again on a higher plane. A person's predicament has to be accepted. Physical suffering is a part of life and people have to cope with it.

Meeting basic needs

Nepal is one of the least developed countries in the world. It has a GNP (see page 105) of only £160 per person compared to £8390 in the UK. Infant mortality is at a rate of 144 deaths per 1000 live births and for those who reach adulthood life expectancy is only 46 years. Only 30 per cent of young children regularly attend primary school and only 10 per cent follow on to secondary school. Low food productivity keeps people short of food with a calorie intake that is 15 per cent less than is needed for them to live a healthy life. The country has few industries. Tourism and earnings sent home or taken home by Gurkha soldiers in the British and Indian armies are the two major sources of foreign earnings. Other countries offer help to Nepal by providing aid in the form of money and technical assistance. India, China, USA and UK are the main donors. With only a small income to use, the government's development programme is to provide the basic needs of the population.

BASIC NEEDS

The things that people need to live a decent life. They include health, education, adequate food, safe water, sanitation, shelter, transport and simple household goods. There are also non-material needs which give a sense of purpose in life such as taking part in decision-making in the community.

Study these developments and attempt the exercises.

Farming

Place these ideas into your order of importance for raising food output of small farmers.
A Provide new strains of crops which give a higher yield than local varieties.
B Bring more land into production by building more terraces on steeper slopes (18).
C Buy tractors and other equipment.
D Plan community projects to bring irrigation water to more fields in the dry season.
E Provide education for farmers to raise output by growing a wider range of crops and to follow summer crops with winter crops.
Give reasons for the order you choose.

Water control schemes

Nepal can only afford to import small amounts of oil, and wood for fuel is in short supply. Heavy monsoon rain and steep mountain slopes offer favourable conditions for generating electricity. Small water control schemes are being built in many places (19).
1 How will electricity benefit people living in towns and villages?
2 What other uses might there be for these water control schemes?

Health

There are 450 doctors and 3000 hospital beds in Nepal to serve a total population of 18 million.

18 Terraces on high slopes

19 Water control scheme

20 A new hospital in the hill and valley region

21 Inside a one-roomed house

In what order of importance would you place these suggestions for improving the health of the Nepalese?
A Train local people to provide basic medical help.
B Build hospitals (20) in every town.
C Lay plastic pipes to carry treated water to villages from water control schemes (19).
D Inoculate all children against TB and other diseases using travelling nurses and helpers.
E Build village health centres to provide a few basic drugs and herbal remedies and provide information on how to prevent illness.
F A latrine-building programme for the whole country.
Give reasons for the order you choose.

Housing

Photograph (21) shows the inside of a one-roomed house for a family of four.
1 Compare this house with your own using these headings: number of rooms, cooking fuels and utensils, water supply, storage of goods, furniture, bed, house decoration.
2 Why might this house be a danger to the health of the family?

Roads

1 What are the problems for road building in large areas of Nepal?

22 A crowded bus on a new road

2 How might a mountain village benefit from having a road and bus service (22) to a town in the hill and valley region? Mention how transport might help the women and children as well as the importance for farming families as a whole.
3 Roads might help disease spread from one village to another. Is this a strong reason for not building roads?

Education

Why will building more schools help the future development of Nepal?

Industry

1 What will be the advantages of setting up many small workshops to produce textiles, for example (23)?
2 Why will being a landlocked country hinder the development of industries for export?

23 A small textile workshop in a village

LEAST DEVELOPED COUNTRIES

The poorest countries in the world. There is little social or economic development. There are low levels of GNP, literacy, food supply and health care with resulting high levels of child mortality, malnutrition and disease. Nepal is one of these countries. Ask for the exercise sheet on the others.

Development links

Explain each of these links:
1. Better education can lead to better health.
2. Better health can lead to increased food supply.
3. Better food supply can lead to longer life expectancy.
4. More food can lead to more children attending school.
5. Better education can lead to increased food supply.
6. Clean water can lead to better health.
7. Cheap supplies of electricity can lead to better health.
8. New roads can lead to development of resources such as minerals.
9. Development of resources can lead to more jobs.

Now explain these connections:

10. More hospitals do not lead to better health if people do not get better food, clean water and better sanitation.
11. Better sanitation such as the latrine programme does not bring better health unless there is better education.
12. Improved housing and clean water are less vital if there has been an improvement in education, health and food supply.

How will this knowledge of development links help a government to decide a programme for providing the basic needs of its people? Are some developments more important than others or do all developments need to take place at the same time?

Tourism

Two hundred thousand tourists visit Nepal every year. Trekkers come to walk the mountain tracks and view the scenery. They might join an organised party and sleep in tented camps or travel on their

24 A wayside lodge

25 Trekkers going uphill, yak herders coming down

own. They can stay at a wayside lodge perhaps for a meal of noodles made on the doorstep (24) and also stay the night. On the trail is where visitors going uphill meet Nepalese sheep and yak herders bringing their wool downhill to the town (25). The trekkers often finish their walks at a mountain base camp where there may be hotels (26) and lodges. It is from here that mountaineers continue the climb to the world's highest peaks.

Another type of tourist can have a less strenuous holiday. They visit the temples and squares of the old towns of Kathmandu, Patan (27) and Bhaktapur in the Kathmandu valley. They can stay in one of the many first-class hotels (28). They make the one-hour flight in a light aircraft to view the Himalayas (2). Another half-hour flight takes the visitor down to the Royal Sitwan national park in the Terai where they can look for one-horned rhinos, Bengal tigers and crocodiles from a safe vantage point on the top of an elephant (29).

FOLLOW-UP WORK

1. List four main reasons why large numbers of tourists visit Nepal each year.
2. Study table (30) which shows advantages and problems which tourism brings to Nepal.
   (a) Do the advantages outweigh the problems? Add your comments.
   (b) Which do you think are the most serious problems and what suggestions can you make to help solve them?
   (c) Why do national parks benefit both the wildlife and the tourist?
3. Explain how the scenes in the following photographs are influenced by tourism:
   (a) photograph (24); (b) photograph (31).

26 Hotel at Annapurna base camp

27 Durbar square in Patan

28 Big hotel in Kathmandu

29 In the Royal Sitwan national park

31 Street scene in Kathmandu

30 Advantages and problems of tourism

ADVANTAGES

1. Tourism provides jobs for porters and guides, in hotels and restaurants (31), trekking agencies and climbing shops, in wayside lodges and for craftsmen and tradesmen, for example.
2. Money from tourism is a major source of foreign currency with which to undertake development projects.
3. Developments made for tourists might help local communities. The roads and airways open up previously isolated areas and the villages located there.
4. Tourists often return to Nepal to offer help to communities where they have stayed. Hospitals and schools, for example, have been built and staffed with people from other countries.

PROBLEMS

1. Cutting down trees to provide fuel for trekking camps and for the lodges, particularly in the high mountains, removes the protective cover of vegetation from a fragile land.
2. Litter scattered by trekkers includes non-degradable cans and plastic bags which pollute the environment.
3. Local people are made more aware of their own poverty in comparison with the wealth exhibited by tourists.
4. Sherpas leave their villages to go on long expeditions. Community life is affected.
5. Tourists may bring disease and the sweets given to children can cause their teeth to decay.

Deforestation and soil erosion

When trekkers stop for a welcome meal at the wayside eating place in the mountains (32) they will notice that the fuel is wood and that the mountainsides in the distance have only a scatter of trees. Wood has to provide the heat for boiling water and cooking meals. It is also used for building and heating most houses in Nepal.

Improvements in health in the last 30 years have resulted in a rapid growth of population (33). This has caused a big increase in the use of wood and half of Nepal's forest has been cut down. Kathmandu with 360 000 people has the biggest demand for wood. The high price of oil makes this alternative source of heat too expensive for people to afford. Woodcutters often trek 20 kilometres carrying wood to the city (34) because all the trees have been stripped from nearby slopes.

With more mouths to feed, more land has been brought under the plough. Trees have been cut down and terraces built on the steep mountain slopes.

An increasing number of animals also take their toll of Nepal's dwindling forests. Sheep, cattle and goats eat young tree saplings and graze the high mountain pastures to the bare soil.

The loss of trees from steep mountain slopes is a national disaster. From the end of June to the middle of September the monsoon can bring four or five days of continuous heavy rain each week. Trees act as a natural protection for the thin soil on steep mountain slopes, and they soak up a huge amount of water and release it back into the air. Their roots keep the soil in place. When the trees are cut down soil erosion takes place at a rapid rate. Terraces and whole hillsides saturated with water become unstable and landslides occur. Photograph (35)

33 Population of Nepal (1961–87)

Year	Population (millions)
1961	9.4
1971	11.6
1981	15.0
1987	17.8

34 Woodcutters carrying logs to Kathmandu

32 Burning wood at a wayside eating place

35 Tourists and porters scramble over a landslide

SOIL EROSION

The removal of soil by wind and rain at a faster rate than it is formed, particularly as a result of man's activities such as cutting down trees and overgrazing pastures. Sheet erosion is the removal of a thin layer of soil. Rill erosion is where water removes soil along little channels a few centimetres deep. Gully erosion is when the water cuts deep channels in the hillside.

shows tourists and porters scrambling over a landslide which blocked the road on which they were travelling. Water streams down slopes cutting deep gullies. Rivers flood because they are carrying greater amounts of water than ever before. They are choked with silt which fills the valley and spreads the floods over a wide area. Photograph (36) shows the gullied slopes and silt-laden river. The rivers flow into the river Ganges which continues on its journey carrying silt to the delta area in Bangladesh. Six billion tonnes of soil are washed from the mountains of Nepal every year in this way. This explains why people say that Nepal's main export is her soil. Thousands of farmers have been forced to leave the mountains because their soil has been washed away.

37 Planting tree seedlings

36 Gullied slopes and silt-laden river

There are schemes to put the trees back onto the hillsides. This is called reafforestation. Photograph (37) shows the land being prepared for the planting of ash seedlings. The area shown in photograph (22) was once gullied by heavy rain but is now planted with a protective cover of young trees.

Village panchayats have set up community projects to plant trees and protect and manage them for the future. Animals are not allowed to graze freely but are confined to stalls. Their manure may be used for biogas (see page 74) and the sludge spread on the fields. Some villages which have depended upon timber cutting for income have been helped to make a living in other ways. They now grow new crops such as tea and learn crafts such as carpet weaving. The carpets can be sold in the towns.

These are just some of the ways the problems of deforestation and soil erosion are being tackled.

A THREE-DIMENSIONAL MODEL

You can construct a three-dimensional model which shows these problems and some solutions. Ask for the model sheet, instructions and follow-up exercises.

TOPIC FOR DISCUSSION

Trees on the slopes or timber for the town (38)?

Bangladesh

A country on a delta

The Ganges (Padma) and Brahmaputra (Jamuna) rivers each flow more than 2500 kilometres from the Himalayan mountains carrying a huge load of sediment to the shallow waters of the Bay of Bengal (1). This silt has built up into the largest river delta in the world and most of it is in Bangladesh.

The Brahmaputra joins the Ganges in Bangladesh forming one river which splits into hundreds of branches (distributaries) each finding its own route to the sea. In this watery landscape boats and bamboo bridges are the best way of getting from one place to another (2).

Every year heavy monsoon rains from June to September, combined with melting snows and downpours in the Himalayas, cause the rivers to flood at least one-third of Bangladesh (3). When the floodwaters go down, a rich layer of silt (alluvium) is left on the fields (4). This rich silt soil and plentiful water combined with tropical heat are ideal conditions for growing paddy rice (5).

1 *Sediment load of some major rivers*

River	Annual load (million tonnes)
Ganges/Brahmaputra	1820
Huang	1600
Amazon	363
Mississippi	300
Nile	111

2 *Boats and bamboo bridges are used*

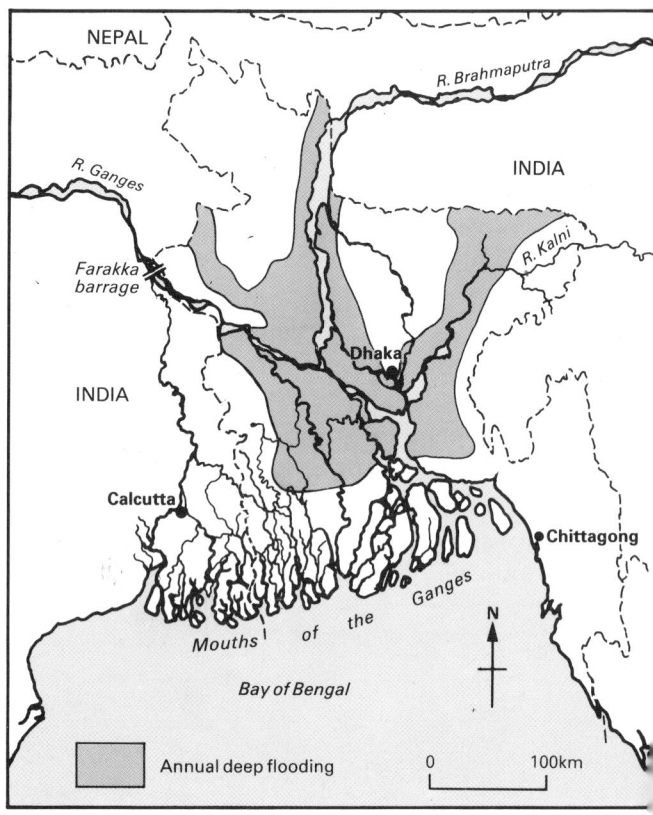

3 *Land is flooded every year in Bangladesh*

4 *Floodwaters leave fresh silt on the fields*

5 *Transplanting rice seedlings to flooded paddy fields*

24 million hit by Bangladesh disaster

14 September 1987

To fly over Bangladesh is to see a drowned world. More than 24 million people are either homeless or without food after the worst floods in the country's history.

The waters began to rise above usual monsoon levels about a month ago and have slowly crept south. Torrential monsoon rain in Bangladesh is only part of the reason for the flood. The main problem is the torrent of water rushing from the Himalayas in Nepal and India. Deforestation in these countries has doubled the amount of water and topsoil running off the Himalayas during the monsoon.

Many Bangladeshis blame India for the scale of the disaster. They believe more water could have been held back by the Farakka barrage on the Ganges river just over the international border.

The death toll has reached 1300. The newest victims are from diarrhoeal diseases such as cholera caused by drinking dirty water. Cholera dehydrates a person so fast, death can come in less than an hour.

The floods have not only destroyed two million bamboo and mud houses but also wiped out the harvest for the coming year. Famine now menaces the people of Bangladesh. Landless labourers will suffer most because there is now no work for them and so they have no money to buy food.

Food aid is being rushed in from the USA and Britain. The food minister says a million tonnes of rice will be distributed in the next two months. This may not reach the hungry millions in the villages because 3000 km of road and 1200 bridges have been destroyed.

The government has received pledges of money as well as food. There is already a programme to protect villages with embankments, houses on mounds and diversion channels to redirect flood water. But all of Bangladesh is so densely settled that the flood water is only directed to another settled area. Bangladesh is just too vulnerable and the problem too vast for any easy solution.

6 Floods in Bangladesh

More than 100 million people are supported on this fertile land. This is six times more people than in Nepal which is a similar size. But in some years the floods have swept through the villages killing thousands of people and scouring the rice crops from the fields. This happened in 1987, as you can read in the newspaper article above (6).

FOLLOW-UP WORK

1 Why do normal floods benefit Bangladesh?
2 Study the newspaper article (6) and answer these questions:
   (a) What were the two main reasons for the floods?
   (b) Why did the floods start in the north and move south?
   (c) Why does Bangladesh hold India partly responsible for the scale of the disaster?
   (d) What were the two reasons why so many people died during the flood?
   (e) Why were more people expected to die many months after the floods?
   (f) Why do landless labourers suffer the most?
   (g) Why were many villages not expected to receive food even though the USA and Britain sent food aid to Bangladesh?
   (h) Why do Bangladesh flood prevention schemes, such as water diversion channels, not solve the problem?
   (i) How can Nepal help to solve the problem?
3 Study news item (8) and answer these questions:
   (a) What was the reason for the flood?
   (b) Why did the flood start in the south and move north?
   (c) Why would this flood leave the land less suitable for farming than the 1987 flood?
   (d) Why do people stay in the coastal danger area?

Now ask for the study sheet on cyclones.

7 House built on a mound

8 Cyclone disaster

26 May 1985

Eleven thousand people are feared dead following yesterday's cyclone which hit the delta area with windspeeds of 130 kmph. The storm surge in the bottleneck area of the Bay of Bengal brought waves 5 metres high which destroyed 17 000 houses and damaged 122 000 more. Coast embankments were washed away and salt water spread over the land and contaminated the wells.

Eight million people live on a thousand islands along this coast. Most are now without food, safe drinking water and fuel. They will stay because the land is fertile, the sea and rivers are rich with fish and there is nowhere else for them to go.

Rich land, poor people

Eighty-two per cent of the people of Bangladesh live in the countryside in 65 000 villages. The land is low, flat and very fertile. Two-thirds of all the land is cultivated. The fields are green with rice most of the year (9) because the tropical monsoon climate makes it possible to grow three crops of rice in one year.

9 Fertile fields of rice

10 Three crop rice farm: circular graphs

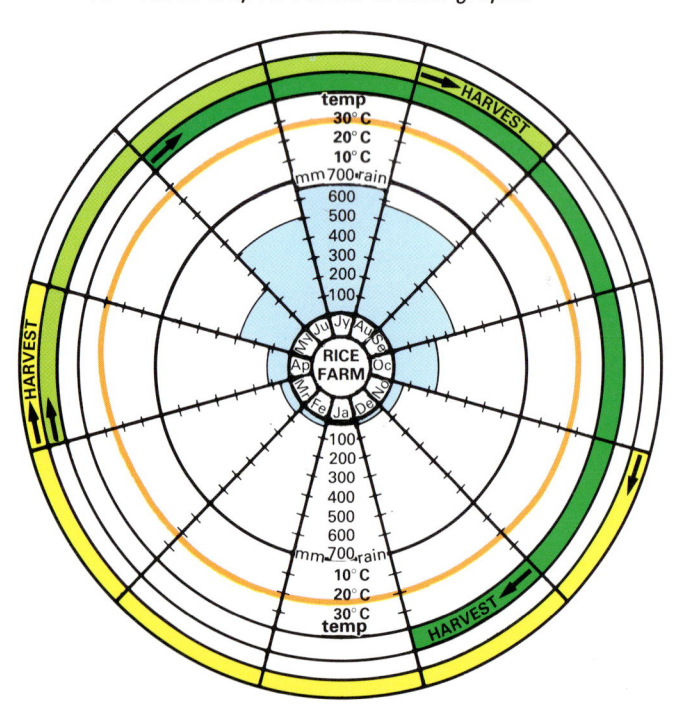

Variety of rice	Millions of hectares	Output in million tonnes
Aus	3	3
Aman	6	8
Boro	2	4

The circular graph (10) shows rainfall amounts and temperatures all the year round and the three varieties of rice which are grown. Study the graph and answer the questions.

1. Why can rice be grown all the year round?
2. Which variety of rice is sown when the early rains, called 'Little Rains', arrive?
3. Which crop grows in flooded fields (5) during the monsoon rains and ripens in the dry season?
4. Which rice crop needs irrigation water?
5. Why might a farmer plant both Aus and Aman varieties of rice?
6. Which rice crop is grown over the widest area of the country?
7. Which crop has the highest yield per hectare?
8. What is the total production of rice in Bangladesh?
9. Look back at your earlier answers and say what might be the easiest way of increasing the total output of rice.
10. Why would the 1987 floods which occurred in September and October (6) be a particular disaster for Bangladeshi rice farmers?

Although the land is fertile, most people in the villages live in absolute poverty. One-quarter of all the children born die before they are five. The children who survive suffer some degree of malnutrition and other diseases which result from not having enough to eat or from a poor diet. This is a world problem. Ask for the information sheet and exercises.

Only 15 per cent of Bangladeshi children have any schooling after the age of eleven. Boys work in the fields (11) and girls work in the home. The older girls help to look after the younger children.

The women look after the home and family. They dehusk the rice using a wooden beam called a dekhi (12) and they prepare the meals. They can spend

11 A boy ploughs his father's field

12 Woman husking rice

hours fetching water, collecting firewood and making clothes. Unlike most other countries, women in Bangladesh die earlier than men, which indicates the hardships they face, including childbearing from an early age. There are many reasons why people live in poverty in Bangladesh. Read about these and answer the questions on the next page.

Too many people and too little land

The population of Bangladesh has risen rapidly in recent years (13). The birth rate is high and the death rate is falling. Most parents expect some of their children to die. They have large families so that some children will survive to look after them in later life. Children also work and are one of the few assets a family has (14). There are six people in the average family.

As the population gets bigger the size of farms gets smaller and the number of landless labourers increases. Thousands of people migrate to Dhaka, the capital city, where they hope to find work in the informal sector pedalling rickshaws (15), hawking or doing casual work. Bangladesh has a problem of overpopulation.

13 Population of Bangladesh (1950–2000)

Year	1950	1960	1970	1980	1987	2000*
Population (millions)	42	52	67	88	107	144
People per km²	290	360	465	610	743	1000

*estimate

OVERPOPULATION

When a country has more people than it can adequately feed either directly by its own food production or indirectly through the use of its other resources, it is overpopulated.

Religion

Eighty-five per cent of the population are Muslims. Religion is the reason this country became separate from the mainly Hindu India. The laws of inheritance say that the father divides his land equally amongst his sons with a half share for daughters. This is the reason most farms are tiny and half are split into six or more plots with little room to turn a plough (11). As Muslims, women usually live in purdah which means they are confined to the home. Divorce is common and women are often left to fend for themselves and the children.

14 Bangladeshi children

15 Street scene in Dhaka

123

Reasons for poverty

Land ownership

In any rural population, food and security for the family depends upon owning land. In Bangladesh one-third of the population has no land and another third has so little land it does not adequately feed the family.

Eight per cent of the population owns half the land. Many landowners hire labourers on a seasonal basis for low wages or let people farm the land in return for half the crops they grow. The landowner is also a money lender who charges high rates of interest on loans to the farmers. When the farmers get in debt they are often forced to sell their small plot to bigger landowners. It is the bigger landowners who have political power at local and national level. They often come from the same families and have a good education. They control the buying and selling of food and can influence government officials.

Colonial rule

Bangladesh has only been an independent country since 1971 following a civil war which separated it from West Pakistan. In 1947, India, and East and West Pakistan gained their independence, having formerly been part of Britain's Indian empire.

Britain's interest in India began in the middle of the eighteenth century in the part of Bengal which is now Bangladesh. At that time the land provided enough food for everyone. Britain changed that by introducing private land ownership and cash crop farming of indigo, tea and jute. Jute is grown in flooded fields (16) and soon began to replace rice over large parts of Bengal.

Raw jute was sent to Britain to be made into hessian sacking, furniture cloth and carpet backing. Britain then began to close down Bengal's cotton weaving industry so that this would not compete with British-made cloth. Today, the imports and exports of Bangladesh (17) show how the pattern established by colonial rule still affects the country. You can see, for example, that cash crops of jute and tea are major exports but wheat and rice have to be imported for everyday survival.

16 Growing jute in flooded fields

17 Composition of trade

Exports (1985)	% of total	Imports (1985)	% of total
Jute and jute products	57	Manufactures	40
Clothing	14	Petroleum	17
Fish	9	Chemicals and medicines	11
Leather	8		
Tea	6	Wheat	5
Others	6	Rice	4
		Others	23

Disasters

We have seen how the monsoon and cyclones bring floods. Floods bring famine. Farmers get into debt and sell their land. They have lost their only sure supply of food and the future security of the family.

FOLLOW-UP WORK

1. How has religion in Bangladesh helped to make small, fragmented farms?
2. Why do flood disasters ruin small farmers but make big landowners more powerful?
3. How did colonial rule help to cause poverty in Bangladesh?
4. Poverty is the main cause of large families rather than large families being the main cause of poverty. How can you explain this idea?
5. Why does a growing population (13) make it very difficult to get rid of poverty?
6. Land reform, which means taking land from big landowners and giving it back to the farmers, is the main hope for reducing poverty. Do you agree? Say why.
7. Why will land reform be difficult to achieve?
8. Although Bangladesh is overpopulated it may not be overpopulated in the future even though there will be more people on the same area of land. How can you explain this?

Aid and development

Bangladesh is perhaps the poorest country in the world and it has a large population to feed. Other countries try to help by sending food, money and technical assistance. This help is called aid and Bangladesh receives more than any other country.

When there is an emergency, such as a flood disaster, the main needs are food, clothing, tents and medical supplies. The women in photograph (18) are making chapattis from wheat flour sent by the USA and Britain during the 1987 flood disaster. This helped to save thousands of people from starvation. Every year Bangladesh receives two million tonnes of food aid. Unfortunately a lot of the food never reaches the people who need it most. Much of it goes to feed the army and police force. Much of it is sold cheaply to people who live in Dhaka and Chittagong. When food does reach the villages it is given out by council officials. They often favour the people who vote for them.

Governments decide to which countries they will give aid. Bangladesh receives over a billion pounds every year. This money helps to pay for projects which should bring long-term development to the country. But some money comes as a loan and Bangladesh is building up debts. The country could be underdeveloping.

UNDERDEVELOPMENT

When a country becomes less able to look after itself it is underdeveloped. A country such as Bangladesh, for example, becomes dependent on aid and could not feed itself without it.

---

18 Emergency food supplies

AID

The help given to a poor country by a richer one (bilateral aid) or from a collection of countries such as the EEC (multilateral aid).

The aid is often sent during or after a disaster (emergency aid). Aid may come in the form of food (food aid) or money to spend on development projects (project aid). Some countries only give aid on the understanding that it is spent on products and services from the donor country (tied aid).

FOLLOW-UP WORK

Imagine that you have to decide how aid money is spent. Your first job is to decide what aid-assisted developments should try to achieve. Here are nine suggestions.

Development aid should achieve the following:

A Help people without making other people poorer than before.
B Help the country that is giving the money as much as the country receiving it.
C Help the poorest people most.
D Bring long-term benefit to the country so that aid will not be needed in the future.
E Help people help themselves.
F Help children become healthy adults.
G Help a country provide the basic needs of food, health and education.
H Help a country develop its land and other resources.
I Help provide the infrastructure (e.g. roads and power supplies) as a basis for social and economic developments.

Put these nine points into order of importance by placing a letter (A to I) onto a number on your own copy of the diamond shown below. Now study the aid-assisted projects on pages 126 and 127. Which three projects would you support? Say why. The projects you choose must meet the requirements at and near the top of your diamond.

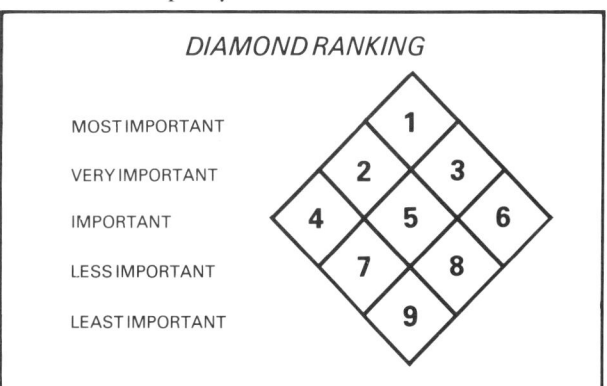

DIAMOND RANKING

MOST IMPORTANT — 1
VERY IMPORTANT — 2, 3
IMPORTANT — 4, 5, 6
LESS IMPORTANT — 7, 8
LEAST IMPORTANT — 9

Development projects in Bangladesh

Project 1: Electricity

Money is to be spent on building pipelines from natural gasfields in the north-east of the country to the largest cities of Dhaka and Chittagong. Power stations in the city will use the gas to generate electricity for homes, business and industry. Factories will also use the gas to make fertilisers to increase farm output.

A national grid will gradually extend out from the city to bring electricity to half of the villages of Bangladesh over a 10-year period. Hydro-electric power produced in the hills east of Chittagong will be fed into the system. The scheme will reduce oil imports which are very expensive.

20 Fish farming for carp and shrimps

19 Working on an irrigation project

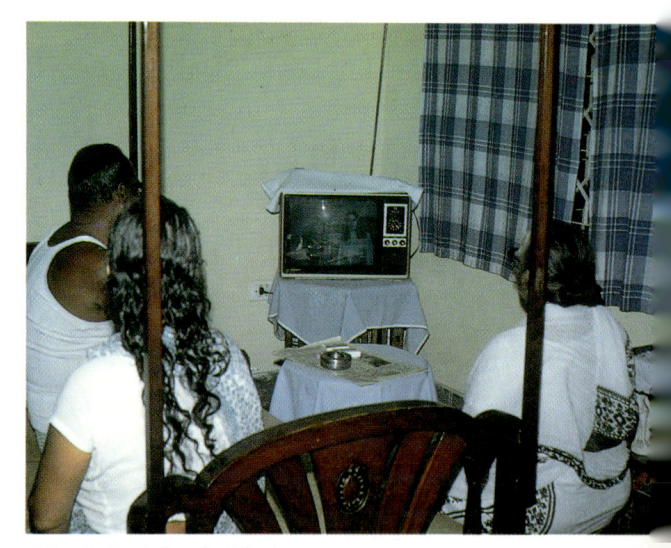

Project 2: Irrigation

Money will provide wages for labourers to dig irrigation channels in many parts of Bangladesh (19). Money will also be needed to provide pumps which can operate when electricity comes to the villages.

Irrigation will increase the production of Boro rice. The channels will have the added benefit of controlling the floodwaters in the monsoon season.

Project 3: Fish farms

Land will be made available to make ponds which will be stocked with fish (20). The fish farms will be run by groups of landless labourers who can repay the costs when they sell the fish in the village. Fish will help to improve the diet of people who eat mainly rice.

Project 4: Communications

Money will be spent on telephone, radio and television services. These will be provided at first in Dhaka (21) spreading later to all parts of the country.

Improved communications will help business and industry. The country will be unified by these new links which will particularly help areas cut off by floods which will now find help in an emergency.

21 Television in Dhaka

Project 5: Embankments

Money is needed to pay wages to landless labourers to build embankments (22) to protect farmland from tidal waves during a cyclone. This will prevent villages from being flooded and stop saltwater polluting the farmland.

Project 6: Road and bridge building

Money will be used to surface the existing road network which at present totals only 6700 kilometres. New roads will also be constructed in rural areas.

A bridge is planned to link Dhaka, the capital city (population 4 million in 1985) with the main port

22 Embankment to protect farmland

Chittagong (1.7 million). These developments will make the villages more accessible to the city markets.

Project 7: Women's groups
Money will help to provide highly trained full-time organisers to set up and run women's groups in collections of villages all over Bangladesh. These groups will provide courses in reading, writing, family planning (23) and children's health. The groups will also learn money-earning crafts (24) and work together to market their products.

23 Receiving family-planning advice

24 Crafts to help the family

Project 8: Rural banks
Money will provide trained bank workers who will set up banks in village communities. The banks will offer low-interest loans to families. They will offer advice on how the money should be used. Some people may want to buy a few animals to fatten, or buy a rickshaw to offer cheap local transport.

Repayments will be spread over the year. Rural banks will give people an alternative to the landowner-moneylender.

WHAT IS DEVELOPMENT?

The study of Bangladesh and many other countries of the developing world has given an insight into the character and culture of nations and into the process of development. This should help you to answer the fundamental question: What is development? Ask for the diamond ranking sheet.

Index

aid 114, 125
alcohol fuel 31
alluvium 120
Amazon forest 36, 39–46, 91
Amazon Indians 45, 46
Andes mountains 6–9
appropriate technology 76
Bangladesh 120–27
basic industries 82
basic needs 8, 114, 116
bauxite mining 43
Bhopal disaster 78
biogas 74, 119
birth and death rates 68, 69, 104, 123
Brasilia 36–39
Brazil 23–46
Calcutta 79–81
capital-intensive 16, 20
car industry 22, 34, 35, 96
Carajas project 43
cash crops 28, 62, 100, 102
caste 72, 81, 113
cattle rearing projects 44–46
Central Business District (CBD) 59, 109
child mortality 57, 104, 112
coffee 26–30
colonialism 84, 99, 124
commercial farming 62, 87
conceptual model 101
copper mining 20, 21, 47–53, 65
core-periphery 14
cyclone 121
Deccan 67, 71, 78
deforestation 43, 44, 78, 117–19
demographic transition 70
development defined 5, 127
Dhaka 125, 127
disease 9, 10, 24, 45, 57, 58, 61, 73, 80, 85, 112, 115
drought 24, 25, 28, 71, 76, 77, 107
ecosystem 41
education 9, 12, 24, 27, 57, 61, 72, 86, 104, 113, 114
employment structure 35
export oriented industry 83, 96
fishing 18, 19, 45, 55, 126
floods 76, 77, 120–25
fragmented farms 9, 73, 76, 78, 87, 123
Ganges river 67, 76–79, 110, 119, 120
green revolution 75, 78
Gross National Product (GNP) 105, 114

growth pole 36
Hausa 98
heavy industry 32, 33, 83
Himalayas 67, 76, 77, 110, 111, 120
hinterland 98, 101
hungry season 56
hydro-electric power (HEP) 33, 43, 63, 65, 107, 114, 126
Ibo 99
import substitution 83, 107
Incas 4
India 67–83
industrial growth stages 32
infant mortality 14, 24, 57, 104, 114
informal sector 13, 31, 60, 123
integrated rural development 88
irrigation 9, 15, 16, 25, 62, 63, 74, 78, 105, 126
Jengka triangle 87, 88
jute 124
Kariba dam 65
Kathmandu 110, 118
Kuala Lumpur 89, 95, 96
labour intensive 7
Lagos 108, 109
land consolidation 76, 78
land reform 9, 25, 112, 124
landlocked countries 48, 49, 98, 110, 115
latifundia 9, 24, 25
least developed countries 115
life expectancy 57, 68, 104, 112, 114, 123
Lima 5, 10–14
linked industries 30, 107
literacy 104, 105
Lusaka 47, 59–61
Malaysia 84–97
malnutrition 8, 68, 85, 112, 122
minifundia 9, 24, 25
monsoon 71, 76–78, 85, 88, 114, 120
multinationals 34, 35, 102
national parks 46, 66, 117
Nepal 110–19
networks and nodes 100, 101
Niger river and delta 98, 100, 102, 107, 109
Nigeria 98–109
oil industry 102–107
overpopulation 123, 124

Panama canal 5
Pan-American Highway 22
Peru 4–22
Peruvian current 15, 18
plantations 15, 24, 26, 62, 63, 84, 87, 88, 91–94
population density 10, 36
poverty 8, 24, 25, 68, 70, 80, 85, 122, 124
primary health care 57
primate city 11, 81, 95
push-pull factors 12
railways 47–49, 100, 101
rainforest 10, 39–46, 84, 87
rainshadow 6, 15, 77
rank order 14, 125
reafforestation 119
regions 5
religion 69, 72, 86, 111, 113, 123
resources 17, 20, 53, 82, 100, 102, 103
rice farming 69, 85–87, 120, 122
Rio de Janeiro 23, 26, 36
road network 7, 36, 40, 106, 115, 127
rubber 91–95
Sahel 98, 107
Sao Paulo 23, 30, 31, 36
savanna 26, 27, 54, 56, 66, 98
shanty towns 13, 14, 31, 60, 79, 80
shifting cultivation 45, 56
shipbuilding 34
site and service schemes 14, 61
slavery 24, 100
soil erosion 41, 44, 78, 118, 119
staple food 8, 45, 55
steel industry 32, 33
subsistence farming 8, 62, 64, 69, 86
Suez canal 53
sugar cane 25, 62, 63
terraces 4, 119
tin mining 89, 90, 95
tourism 116, 117
Trans–Amazonian Highway 40, 41, 46
underdevelopment 125
urbanisation 31
vicious circles 68
village life 8, 9, 45, 54–58, 71–76, 85, 122, 123
wildlife 66, 117
Yoruba 99, 108
Zambia 47–66

128